Great Meals in Minutes was created by
Rebus, Inc.
and published by Time-Life Books.

Rebus, Inc.

Publisher: Rodney Friedman
Editorial Director: Shirley Tomkievicz

Editor: Marya Dalrymple
Art Director: Ronald Gross
Senior Editor: Charles Blackwell
Food Editor and Food Stylist: Grace Young
Photographer: Steven Mays
Prop Stylist: Cathryn Schwing
Staff Writer: Alexandra Greeley
Associate Editor: Bonnie J. Slotnick
Assistant Food Stylist: Karen Hatt
Recipe Tester: Gina Palombi Barclay
Production Assistants: Lorna Bieber,
Lisa Young

For information about any Time-Life book,
please write:
Reader Information
Time-Life Books
541 North Fairbanks Court
Chicago, Illinois 60611

Library of Congress Cataloging in Publication Data
Make-ahead menus.
   (Great meals in minutes)
   Includes index.
   1. Cookery.   2. Menus.   3. Cooks—United States
Biography.   I. Time-Life Books   II. Series.
TX652.M249   1986   641.5′55   85-16560
ISBN 0-86706-298-3 (lib. bdg.)
ISBN 0-86706-297-5 (retail ed.)

First printing. Printed in U.S.A.
Published simultaneously in Canada.
School and library distribution by Silver Burdett
Company, Morristown, New Jersey.

TIME-LIFE is a trademark of Time Incorporated
U.S.A.

Time-Life Books Inc.
is a wholly owned subsidiary of
Time Incorporated
Founder: Henry R. Luce 1898–1967
Editor-in-Chief: Henry Anatole Grunwald
President: J. Richard Munro
Chairman of the Board: Ralph P. Davidson
Corporate Editor: Jason McManus
Group Vice President, Books: Reginald K.
Brack Jr.
Vice President, Books: George Artandi

Time-Life Books Inc.

Editor: George Constable
Executive Editor: George Daniels
Editorial General Manager: Neal Goff
Director of Design: Louis Klein
Editorial Board: Dale M. Brown, Roberta
Conlan, Ellen Phillips, Gerry Schremp,
Donia Ann Steele, Rosalind Stubenberg,
Kit van Tulleken, Henry Woodhead
Director of Research: Phyllis K. Wise
Director of Photography: John Conrad Weiser

President: William J. Henry
Senior Vice President: Christopher T. Linen
Vice Presidents: Stephen L. Bair, Edward
Brash, John M. Fahey Jr., Juanita T. James,
James L. Mercer, Wilhelm R. Saake, Paul R.
Stewart, Leopoldo Toralballa

Editorial Operations
Design: Ellen Robling (assistant director)
Copy Chief: Diane Ullius
Editorial Operations: Caroline A. Boubin
(manager)
Production: Celia Beattie
Quality Control: James J. Cox (director)
Library: Louise D. Forstall

SERIES CONSULTANT
Margaret E. Happel is the author of *Ladies'
Home Journal Adventures in Cooking,
Ladies' Home Journal Handbook of Holiday
Cuisine,* and other best-selling cookbooks, as
well as the translator and adapter of Rebecca
Hsu Hiu Min's *Delights of Chinese Cooking.* A
food consultant based in New York City, she
has been director of the food department of
Good Housekeeping and editor of *American
Home* magazine.

WINE CONSULTANT
Tom Maresca combines a full-time career
teaching English literature with writing
about and consuming fine wines. He is the
author of *Mastering Wine a Taste at a Time.*

Cover: Marie Simmons's *panzanella,* loin of
pork with rosemary and garlic, and roasted
bell peppers and onions. See pages 66–67.

Great Meals
IN MINUTES
MAKE-AHEAD
MENUS

TIME-LIFE BOOKS, ALEXANDRIA, VIRGINIA

Contents

Meet the Cooks

JENIFER HARVEY LANG

Food writer and professional cook Jenifer Harvey Lang, a graduate of the Culinary Institute of America, was the first woman to cook at the "21" Club in New York City. She writes a monthly column, "Foreign Affairs," for *European Travel and Life* magazine and is the author of *Tastings*, a rated guide to the forty most important staples in the American pantry.

MARILYN HANSEN

Marilyn Hansen, who studied cooking with Dione Lucas and James Beard, has worked as assistant food editor at *McCall's* magazine and as food editor of *Family Weekly*. She is currently a food and beverage writer and consultant to *USA Weekend* and is a member of Les Dames d'Escoffier and The Newswomen's Club of New York.

MARGARET FRASER

Home economist Margaret Fraser lives in Toronto, Canada, where she manages her own consulting business, specializing in food styling for magazines, television commercials, and product packaging. She is also associate food editor at *Canadian Living* magazine.

ROBERTA RALL

Roberta Rall works as a freelance food stylist and home economist. She prepares and styles food for photography for numerous publications, including cookbooks and publicity releases; develops recipes for specific food products and audiences; and organizes taste tests.

GLORIA ZIMMERMAN

A noted authority on Chinese, Southeast Asian, and French cuisines, Gloria Zimmerman is co-author of *The Classic Cuisine of Vietnam* and was a consulting editor for *The Encyclopedia of Chinese Cooking* and *The Encyclopedia of Asian Cooking*. Besides running her own cooking school, she has taught cooking at many department stores and gourmet shops nationwide, and also for the Yale in China program. She also conducts gastronomic tours to the provinces of France.

MARIE SIMMONS

After studying food and nutrition at Pratt Institute, Marie Simmons went on to spend ten years working in the test kitchen at *Woman's Day* magazine. She has also been a pastry chef, managed a food service operation, and was responsible for all recipe development at *Cuisine* magazine. At present, she is a freelance consultant.

PENELOPE CASAS

Having lived in Spain for many years, Penelope Casas visits that country annually to add to her collection of regional recipes. She has written about travel and food for the *New York Times*, *Vogue*, and *Food & Wine*, and now teaches at the New York Cooking Center and lectures at New York University. She is the author of *The Foods and Wines of Spain* and *Tapas: The Little Dishes of Spain*.

SUSAN WYLER

Originally from Connecticut, Susan Wyler lives and works in New York City, where she is an associate editor at *Food & Wine* magazine. A self-taught cook who has also studied with James Beard, Madeleine Kamman, and Grace Chu, she has run her own catering firm, worked as an editor on the Betty Crocker cookbooks, and contributed food articles to national publications. In addition, she is the author of the cookbook *Tailgate Parties*.

MICHAEL McLAUGHLIN

Born and raised in Colorado, food writer and professional cook Michael McLaughlin owned a catering company and cooking school there before moving to the East Coast. He has managed The Silver Palate, a specialty foods company in New York City, was co-author of *The Silver Palate Cookbook*, and has contributed numerous articles to national food publications. At present, he is co-owner and chef of The Manhattan Chili Co., a restaurant in Greenwich Village.

Make-Ahead Menus in Minutes
GREAT MEALS FOR FOUR IN AN HOUR OR LESS

For many cooks, preparing an entire meal—even one that takes only an hour—at the end of a hectic day is a chore rather than an enjoyable experience. There is hardly anything more agitating than rushing from the office or the gym or a child's school to the supermarket and then home to beat the clock before guests arrive. Often the amenities of fine dining—flowers, an attractive table setting, creative garnishes, or music—are sacrificed for lack of time.

In using this volume, you will discover that preplanning and precooking entire meals or parts of meals can prevent last-minute chaos in the kitchen. You will be free to relax with family and friends, and you will have the time to indulge in some of the more creative aspects of entertaining. You will also find that a make-ahead meal need not be the expected marinated chicken or macaroni casserole. A surprising variety of international dishes—including *bouillabaisse* and beef Stroganoff—lend themselves to advance preparation. In fact, the flavors of many make-ahead dishes improve upon standing.

A good number of the main courses, side dishes, and desserts in this volume can be prepared a full 24 hours before serving. Some more delicate recipes, such as fish in parchment or *spanakopita*, are best made on the day of serving. The time-consuming work—washing and tearing salad greens, trimming and cutting up vegetables and meats, and making salad dressings—is done in advance. All you may have to do during the 30 minutes before mealtime is reheat dishes if necessary, put on the final touches, or prepare a simple dish such as rice (which does not usually reheat well) from scratch. The total time you spend in the kitchen is only an hour and a half, and because the last half hour is not complicated, you will come to the table relaxed. The start-to-finish steps for each menu indicate what to do in advance and what must be done just before serving.

On the following pages, nine of America's most talented cooks present 27 complete menus featuring ideas for make-ahead meals, from an elegant roast loin of pork with bell peppers served at room temperature to a simple supper of Swedish meatballs and cucumber and radish salad. There are recipes for Thai, Vietnamese, Hungarian, French, Italian, and Spanish dishes, many of which work as lunches or brunches as well as dinners.

Each menu serves four people, and the cooks focus on a new kind of American cuisine that not only borrows ideas and techniques from around the world but also values our native traditions. They use fresh produce, with no powdered sauces or other dubious shortcuts. The other ingredients called for (vinegars, spices, herbs, and so on) are all of very high quality and are usually available in supermarkets or specialty food stores.

The cooks and the kitchen staff have meticulously planned and tested the menus for appearance as well as for taste, as the accompanying photographs show: The vegetables are brilliant and fresh, the visual combinations appetizing. The table settings feature bright colors, simple flower arrangements, and attractive but not necessarily expensive serving dishes.

For each menu, the Editors, with advice from the cooks, suggest wines and other beverages. And there are suggestions for the use of leftovers and for complementary dishes and desserts. On each menu page, you will find a number of other tips, from an easy method for working with filo to advice for selecting fresh produce.

BEFORE YOU START

Great Meals in Minutes is designed for efficiency and ease. This book will work best for you if you follow these suggestions:

1. Refresh your memory with the few simple cooking techniques on the following pages. They will quickly become second nature, and you will produce professional-quality meals in minutes.

2. Read the menus before you shop. Each lists the ingredients in the order that you would expect to shop for them. Many items will already be on your pantry shelf.

3. Check the equipment list on page 11. Good sharp knives and pots and pans of the right shape and material are essential for making great meals in minutes. This may be the time to buy a few things: The right equipment can turn cooking from a necessity into a creative experience.

4. Set out everything you need before you start to cook. The lists at the beginning of each menu tell just what is required. To save effort, always keep your ingredients in the same place so you can reach for them instinctively.

5. Follow the start-to-finish steps for each menu. That way you will save yourself time and effort.

Ready for the table: Susan Wyler's creamy carrot soup and cold beef salad (see page 88). Preparing a meal such as this the day before or the morning of serving gives you plenty of time to relax before the guests arrive.

TO MAKE YOUR MEALS EXTRA SPECIAL

It is the special touches that take a meal beyond the ordinary. By cooking in advance, you should have some extra time to devote to such often-neglected refinements as making garnishes and setting a pretty table.

Carved Vegetables

One of the most dramatic ways to embellish a plate is to carve vegetables for garnishes. The only tool you need is a sharp paring knife. The following garnishes are used in this volume:

Tomato roses: A tomato rose is one of the easiest garnishes to make. Select small tomatoes. **(1)** Using a sharp paring knife and starting at the stem end, cut a thin slice from the top of the tomato, being careful not to sever it completely. **(2)** Continue to peel the skin of the tomato in a long continuous strip about ½ inch wide (depending on the size of the tomato), rotating the tomato as you cut to follow its curve. **(3)** Remove as much flesh as possible from the strip of skin. **(4)** To form the blossom, begin at the tip of the strip and roll it around itself in spiral fashion up to the first slice (which becomes the base). **(5)** Place the blossom on the base, then flare the blossom slightly to resemble rose petals. See the illustrations at left below and Roberta Rall's Menu 1, page 46.

Radish mushrooms: In this garnish, radishes are cut to resemble mushrooms. **(1)** Select large firm radishes; slice off the stems and leaves and long root ends. **(2)** With a sharp paring knife, make a cut about ¼ inch deep completely around the center of each radish. **(3)** Neatly cut away some of the flesh from the leaf end to the center incision to make a stem about ½ inch thick. Cut off a thin slice from the bottom of the stem to square it, if necessary. See the illustrations that follow and Penelope Casas's Menu 1, page 76.

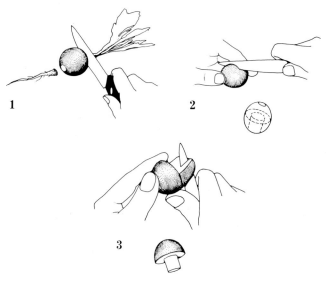

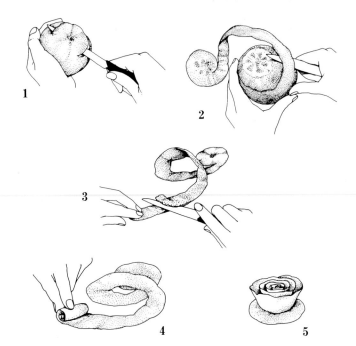

Cucumber fans: For four fans, select a large firm cucumber. Do not peel it. **(1)** Slice off both ends, leaving a 4-inch center section. **(2)** Slicing lengthwise, cut off a third of this section to use for the fans. (Reserve the rest of the cucumber for another use.) **(3)** Place the section of cucumber flat-side down and cut it crosswise into four 1-inch-wide sections. Next, make four equally spaced cuts lengthwise in each section, leaving a narrow strip uncut at the top to hold the section together. Soak the sections in a salt solution (1 tablespoon salt to 1 quart water) for 10 minutes so they will be pliable enough to bend. **(4)** Fold the first four strips of each section over to make the fan, leaving the last strip straight. See the illustrations that follow and Marilyn Hansen's Menu 3, page 31.

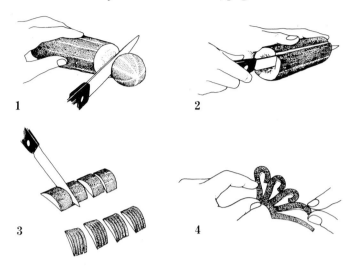

Folded Napkins

Whether you are serving a family meal or an elegant dinner for company, decoratively folded napkins help to make a table more distinctive. Traditionally, the napkin is placed to the left of the fork or in the center of the plate, in a rectangular shape for dinner or in a triangle for lunch. However, a napkin is just as appropriate, and more interesting, when folded into an attractive shape and placed anywhere you like—in a goblet or glass, above the plate, or even to the right of the spoon. A 17- or 20-inch-square napkin in a washable fabric such as linen, cotton, or a cotton blend is ideal for making folds, although a large good-quality paper napkin is also suitable for certain folds. Solid-color napkins seem to look better than printed ones when folded. For the best results, be sure the napkin is square and not limp. If you are using a cloth napkin, starch it lightly to give it extra body, then iron it to remove any creases before you begin folding. The following napkin folds are easy to achieve with a little practice:

The fan: This napkin looks lovely in a glass or a napkin ring. Fold the napkin in half to form a rectangle with the fold at the bottom. Accordion-pleat the rectangle, starting at one short side, making 1-inch pleats. Place the bottom of the fan in a glass or in a napkin ring and let the pleats fan out.

The cone: (1) Fold the napkin into quarters. (2) Place the napkin so the open points are on the upper right. (3) To form the cone, start rolling tightly from the bottom-left corner toward the upper right, keeping the point of the cone at the left and tightly rolled. (4) The upper-left corner becomes the point of the cone and the open end will be on the right. (5) Turn the cone wide-end up, forming a cuff on the outside to hold the cone together. Stand the folded napkin upright. See the illustrations that follow.

Buffet servers: (1) Fold the napkin into quarters. (2) Place the napkin so the open points are at the upper left.

(3) Fold the upper-left corner of the top layer down to the lower-right corner. (4) Fold under the top-right and bottom-left corners. (5) Place silverware in the pocket. See the illustrations below.

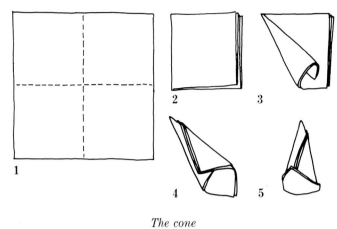

The cone

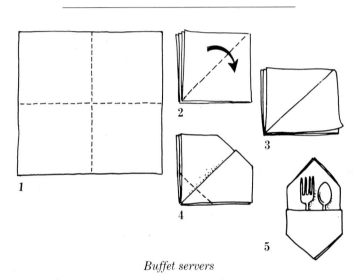

Buffet servers

GENERAL COOKING TECHNIQUES

Sautéing

Sautéing is a form of quick frying with no cover on the pan. In French, *sauter* means "to jump," which is what vegetables or small pieces of food do when you shake the sauté pan. The purpose is to brown the food lightly and seal in the juices, sometimes before further cooking. This technique has three critical elements: the right pan, the proper temperature, and dry food.

The sauté pan: A proper sauté pan is 10 to 12 inches in diameter and has 2- to 3-inch straight sides that allow you to turn the food and still keep the fat from spattering. It has a heavy bottom that can be moved back and forth across a burner easily. The best material (and the most expensive) for a sauté pan is tin-lined copper because it is a superior heat conductor. Heavy-gauge aluminum works well but will discolor acidic foods like tomatoes. Therefore, you should not use aluminum if acidic food is to be cooked for more than 20 minutes. Be sure to buy a sauté pan with a tight-fitting cover. Make certain the handle is long and is comfortable to hold. Use a wooden spatula or tongs to keep the food moving in the pan as you shake it over the burner. If the food sticks, a metal spatula will loosen it best. Turn the food so that all surfaces come into contact with the hot fat.

Never immerse the hot pan in cold water because this will warp the metal. Allow the pan to cool slightly, then add water and let it sit until you are ready to wash it.

The fat: Half butter and half vegetable or peanut oil is perfect for most sautéing: It heats to high temperatures without burning, yet allows a rich butter flavor. For cooking, unsalted butter tastes best and adds no extra salt.

Some sautéing recipes in this book call for olive oil, which imparts a delicious and distinctive flavor of its own and is less sensitive than butter to high heat. Nevertheless, even the finest olive oil has some residue of fruit pulp, which will occasionally scorch. Watch carefully when you sauté in olive oil; discard any scorched oil and start with fresh if necessary.

To sauté properly, heat the fat until it is hot but not smoking. When you see small bubbles on top of the fat, lower the heat because the fat is on the verge of smoking. When using butter and oil together, add butter to the hot oil. After the foam from the melting butter subsides, you are ready to sauté. If the temperature of the fat is just right, the food will sizzle when you put it in the pan. Marie Simmons sautés sausage, page 72.

Stir Frying

This technique requires very little oil, and the foods—which you stir continuously—fry quickly over very high heat. Stir frying is ideal for cooking bite-size, shredded, or thinly sliced portions of vegetables, fish, meat, or poultry, alone or in combination. In her menu 1, page 57, Gloria Zimmerman stir fries chicken.

Braising

Braising is simmering meats or vegetables in a relatively small amount of liquid, usually for a long period of time. Sometimes the food is browned or parboiled before braising. You may wish to flavor the braising liquid with herbs, spices, or aromatic vegetables, or use wine, stock, or tomato sauce as a medium. Marie Simmons braises veal and vegetables on page 69.

Deglazing

This is an easy way to create a sauce for sautéed, braised, or roasted food. To deglaze, pour off all but 1 to 2 tablespoons of fat from the pan in which the food has been cooked. Add liquid—water, wine, or stock—and reduce the sauce over medium heat, using a wooden spoon to scrape up and blend the concentrated juices and browned bits of food clinging to the bottom of the pan into the sauce. Susan Wyler uses this technique in her recipe for Chicken with Olives and Sun-Dried Tomatoes, page 93.

Blanching

Blanching, or parboiling, is an invaluable technique. Immerse vegetables for a few minutes in boiling water, then refresh them, that is, plunge them into cold water to stop their cooking and set their colors. Blanching softens or tenderizes dense or crisp vegetables, often as a preliminary to further cooking by another method, such as stir frying. On page 49, Roberta Rall blanches tomatoes.

Broiling and Grilling

In broiling, the food cooks directly under the heat source. In grilling, the food cooks either directly over an open fire or on a well-seasoned cast-iron griddle placed over a burner. Margaret Fraser broils lamb kabobs, page 37.

Poaching

You poach meat, fish, chicken, fruit, or eggs in very hot liquid in a pan on top of the stove. You can use water, or better still, beef, chicken, or fish stock, or a combination of stock and white wine, or even cream as the poaching liquid. On page 60, Gloria Zimmerman poaches chicken for a Vietnamese meal.

Making Chicken Stock

Although canned chicken broth or stock is all right for emergencies, homemade chicken stock has a rich flavor that is hard to match. Moreover, the commercial broths—particularly the canned ones—are likely to be oversalted.

To make your own stock, save chicken parts as they accumulate and put them in a bag in the freezer; then have a rainy-day stock-making session using one of the recipes below. The skin from a yellow onion will add color; the optional veal bone will add extra flavor and richness.

3 pounds bony chicken parts, such as wings, back, and neck
1 veal knuckle (optional)
3 quarts cold water
1 yellow unpeeled onion, stuck with 2 cloves
2 stalks celery with leaves, cut in 2
12 crushed peppercorns
2 carrots, scraped and cut into 2-inch lengths
4 sprigs parsley
1 bay leaf
1 tablespoon fresh thyme, or 1 teaspoon dried
Salt (optional)

1. Wash chicken parts and veal knuckle (if you are using it) and drain. Place in large soup kettle or stockpot (any big pot) with the remaining ingredients—except salt. Cover pot and bring to a boil over moderate heat.

2. Lower heat and simmer stock, partly covered, 2 to 3 hours. Skim foam and scum from top of stock several times. Add salt to taste after stock has cooked 1 hour.

3. Strain stock through fine sieve placed over large bowl. Discard chicken pieces, vegetables, and seasonings. Let stock cool uncovered (this will speed cooling process). When completely cool, refrigerate. Fat will rise and congeal conveniently at top. You may skim it off and discard it or leave it as protective covering for stock.

Yield: About 10 cups

Equipment

Proper cooking equipment makes the work light and is a good cook's most prized possession. You can cook expertly without a store-bought steamer or even a food processor, but basic pans, knives, and a few other items are indispensable. Below are the things you need—and some attractive options—for preparing the menus in this volume.

Pots and pans

2 large kettles or stockpots, with covers

3 skillets (large, medium, small) with covers; one with oven-proof handle

3 saucepans with covers (1-, 2-, and 4-quart capacities)
  Choose heavy-gauge enameled cast-iron, plain cast-iron, aluminum-clad stainless steel, or aluminum (but you need at least one saucepan that is not aluminum). Best—but very expensive—is tin-lined copper.

Wok

Roasting pan with rack

Broiler pan with rack

Medium-size shallow baking dish

Two 17 x 11-inch baking sheets

Small baking sheet

9-inch glass pie plate

Jelly-roll pan

Flameproof casserole with cover

Salad bowl

Four individual casseroles or gratin dishes

Knives

A carbon-steel knife takes a sharp edge but tends to rust. You must wash and dry it after each use; otherwise it can blacken foods and counter tops. Good-quality stainless-steel knives, frequently honed, are less trouble and will serve just as well in the home kitchen. Never put a fine knife in the dishwasher. Rinse it, dry it, and put it away—but not loose in a drawer. Knives will stay sharp if they have their own storage rack.

Small paring knife

10-inch chef's knife

Bread knife (serrated edge)

Sharpening steel

Other cooking tools

2 sets of mixing bowls in graduated sizes, one set preferably glass or stainless steel

Flour sifter

Colander with a round base (stainless steel, aluminum, or enamel)

2 sets of measuring cups and spoons in graduated sizes
  One for dry ingredients, another for shortenings and liquids.

Strainer

Slotted spoon

Long-handled wooden spoons

Ladle

Slotted spatula

2 metal spatulas or turners (for lifting hot foods from pans)

Rubber or vinyl spatula (for folding in ingredients)

Grater (metal, with several sizes of holes)
  A rotary grater is handy for hard cheese.

Wire whisk

Pair of metal tongs

Wooden board

Garlic press

Vegetable peeler

Vegetable brush

Stiff-bristled brush

Collapsible vegetable steamer

Mortar and pestle

Pastry brush for basting (a small, new paintbrush that is not nylon serves well)

Meat thermometer

Melon baller

Cooling rack

Kitchen shears

Kitchen timer

Cheesecloth

Aluminum foil

Paper towels

Plastic wrap

Plastic bags

Waxed paper

Kitchen string

Oven mitts or potholders

Small paper bag

Electric appliances

Food processor or blender
  A blender will do most of the work required in this volume, but a food processor will do it more quickly and in larger volume. A food processor should be considered a necessity, not a luxury, for anyone who enjoys cooking.

Electric mixer

Optional cooking tools

Salad spinner

Small jar with tight-fitting lid

Spice grinder

Salad servers

Citrus juicer
  Inexpensive glass kind from the dime store will do.

Nutmeg grater

Deep-fat thermometer

Roll of masking tape or white paper tape for labeling and dating

Pantry (for this volume)

A well-stocked, properly organized pantry is essential for preparing great meals in the shortest time possible. Whether your pantry consists of a small refrigerator and two or three shelves over the sink, or a large freezer, refrigerator, and entire room just off the kitchen, you must protect staples from heat and light.

In maintaining your pantry, follow these rules:

1. Store staples by kind and date. Canned goods, canisters, and spices need a separate shelf, or a separate spot on a shelf. Date all staples—shelved, refrigerated, or frozen—by writing the date directly on the package or on a bit of masking tape. Then put the oldest ones in front to be sure you use them first.

2. Store flour, sugar, and other dry ingredients in canisters or jars with tight lids. Glass and clear plastic allow you to see at a glance how much remains.

3. Keep a running grocery list so that you can note when a staple is half gone, and be sure to stock up.

ON THE SHELF:

Anchovies
Anchovy fillets, both flat and rolled, come oil-packed in tins.

Capers
Capers are usually packed in vinegar and less frequently in salt. If you use the latter, you should rinse them under cold water before using them.

Cornstarch
Less likely to lump than flour, cornstarch is an excellent thickener for sauces. Substitute in the following proportions: 1 tablespoon cornstarch to 2 of flour.

Flour
all-purpose, bleached or unbleached

Garlic
Store in a cool, dry, well-ventilated place. Garlic powder and garlic salt are not adequate substitutes for fresh garlic.

Herbs and spices
The flavor of fresh herbs is much better than that of dried. Fresh herbs should be refrigerated and used as soon as possible. The following herbs are perfectly acceptable dried, but buy in small amounts, store airtight in dry area away from heat and light, and use as quickly as possible. In measuring herbs, remember that one part dried will equal three parts fresh. Crushing dried herbs brings out their flavor: Use a mortar and pestle or sandwich the herbs between 2 sheets of waxed paper and crush with a rolling pin. *Note:* Dried chives and parsley should not be on your shelf, since they have little or no flavor; frozen chives are acceptable. Buy whole spices rather than ground, as they keep their flavor much longer. Grind spices at home and store as directed for herbs.

basil
bay leaves
caraway seeds
Cayenne pepper
cinnamon
coriander, ground
curry powder
nutmeg, whole and ground
oregano
paprika, sweet Hungarian
pepper
  black peppercorns
  These are unripe peppercorns dried in their husks. Grind with a pepper mill for each use.
  white peppercorns
  These are the same as the black variety, but are picked ripe and husked. Use them in pale sauces when black pepper specks would spoil the appearance.
red pepper flakes (also called crushed red pepper)
rosemary
saffron
  Made from the dried stigmas of a species of crocus, this spice—the most costly of all seasonings—adds both color and flavor. Use sparingly.
salt
  Use coarse salt—commonly available as kosher or sea—for its superior flavor, texture, and purity. Kosher salt and sea salt are less salty than table salt. Substitute in the following proportions: three-quarters teaspoon table salt equals just under one teaspoon kosher or sea salt.
tarragon
thyme

Hot pepper sauce

Nuts, whole, chopped, or slivered
pine nuts (pignoli)
walnuts

Oils
corn, safflower, peanut, or vegetable
  Because these neutral-tasting oils have high smoking points, they are good for high-heat sautéing.
olive oil
  Sample French, Greek, Spanish, and Italian oils. Olive oil ranges in color from pale yellow to dark green and in taste from mild and delicate to rich and fruity. Different olive oils can be used for different purposes: for example, use stronger ones for cooking, lighter ones for salads. The finest quality olive oil is labeled extra-virgin or virgin.

Olives
California pitted black olives

Onions
Store all dry-skinned onions in a cool, dry, well-ventilated place.
red or Italian onions
  Zesty tasting and generally eaten raw. The perfect salad onion.
shallots
  The most subtle member of the onion family, the shallot has a delicate garlic flavor.
yellow onions
  All-purpose cooking onions, strong in taste.

Potatoes, boiling and baking
  "New" potatoes are not a particular kind of potato, but any potato that has not been stored.

Rice
long-grain white rice
  Slender grains that become light and fluffy when cooked and are best for general use.

Soy sauce, dark

Stock, chicken and beef
  For maximum flavor and quality, your own stock is best (see recipe page 10), but canned stock, or broth, is adequate for most recipes and convenient to have on hand.

Sugar
granulated sugar
brown sugar

Tomatoes
Italian plum tomatoes
Canned plum tomatoes (preferably imported) are an acceptable substitute for fresh.

Vinegars
balsamic vinegar
distilled white vinegar
rice vinegar
red and white wine vinegars
sherry vinegar

Wines and spirits
white wine, dry

Worcestershire sauce

IN THE REFRIGERATOR:

Basil
Though fresh basil is widely available only in summer, try to use it whenever possible to replace dried; the flavor is markedly superior. Stand the stems, preferably with roots intact, in a jar of water, and loosely cover leaves with a plastic bag.

Bread crumbs
You need never buy bread crumbs. To make fresh crumbs, use fresh or day-old bread and process in food processor or blender. For dried, toast bread 30 minutes in preheated 250-degree oven, turning occasionally to prevent slices from browning. Proceed as for fresh. Store bread crumbs in an airtight container: fresh crumbs in the refrigerator and dried crumbs in a cool, dry place. Either type may also be frozen for several weeks in a tightly sealed plastic bag.

Butter
Many cooks prefer unsalted butter because of its finer flavor and because it does not burn as easily as salted.

Cheese
Goat cheese
Goat cheese, or *chèvre*, has a distinct tanginess, though it is quite mild when young. Domestic goat cheeses are less salty than the imported types.

Mozzarella
A mild cheese, most commonly made from cow's milk. Fresh mozzarella is far superior to packaged and can generally be found in Italian grocery stores.

Parmesan cheese
Avoid the pre-grated packaged variety; it is very expensive and almost flavorless. Buy Parmesan by the quarter- or half-pound wedge and grate as needed: 4 ounces yields about one cup of grated cheese.

Chives
Refrigerate fresh chives wrapped in plastic. You may also buy small pots of growing chives—keep them on a windowsill and snip as needed.

Coriander
Also called *cilantro* or Chinese parsley, its pungent leaves resemble flat-leaf parsley. Keep in a glass of water covered with a plastic bag.

Cream
half-and-half
heavy cream
sour cream

Eggs
Will keep 4 to 5 weeks in refrigerator. For best results, bring to room temperature before using, except when separating.

Ginger, fresh
Found in the produce section. Wrap in a paper towel, then in plastic, and refrigerate; it will keep for about 1 month, but should be checked weekly for mold. Or, if you prefer, store it in the freezer, where it will last about 3 months. Firm, smooth-skinned ginger need not be peeled.

Lemons
In addition to its many uses in cooking, a slice of lemon rubbed over cut apples and pears will keep them from discoloring. Do not substitute bottled juice or lemon extract.

Limes

Milk

Mint
Fresh mint will keep for a week if wrapped in a damp paper towel and enclosed in a plastic bag.

Mustards
The recipes in this book usually call for Dijon or coarse-grained mustard.

Parsley
The two most commonly available kinds of parsley are flat-leaf and curly; they can be used interchangeably when necessary. Flat-leaf parsley has a more distinctive flavor and is generally preferred in cooking. Curly parsley wilts less easily and is excellent for garnishing. Store parsley in a glass of water and cover loosely with a plastic bag. It will keep for a week in the refrigerator. Or wash and dry it, and refrigerate in a small plastic bag with a dry paper towel inside to absorb any moisture.

Scallions
Also called green onions. Mild flavor. Use the white bulbs as well as the fresh green tops. Wrap in plastic and store in the refrigerator, or chop coarsely, wrap in plastic, and freeze.

Yogurt

Jenifer Harvey Lang

MENU 1 (Right)
Brigand's Brochettes
Baked Brussels Sprouts
Radish Salad

MENU 2
Fish Schnitzel
Steamed Parslied Potatoes
Red and Green Cabbage Salad

MENU 3
Baked Fish with Pecan Stuffing
Cauliflower, Bell Pepper, and Olive Salad

Jenifer Lang says that over the years she has come to prefer "down-to-earth cooking that leaves guests full and immensely satisfied." After marrying restaurateur George Lang and traveling with him to his native Hungary, she discovered that the cuisine of that country particularly suited her taste. All three of her menus typify meals you might eat in Middle European homes, and all can be prepared the day before or the day of serving. The main dishes go directly from the refrigerator into the broiler, oven, or frying pan.

Menu 1 features brigand's brochettes, reputedly created long ago by Hungarian robbers who never stayed in one place long enough to cook anything more complex than grilled meats and vegetables. If you wish, serve the brochettes in traditional Hungarian style by balancing the skewers atop thick slices of deep-fried bread. Baked Brussels sprouts with sour cream and radish salad are the accompaniments.

Schnitzel made with ground fish is the focus of Menu 2. The fish is shaped into patties, coated with egg and bread crumbs, and then refrigerated. Just before serving, the patties are fried to a golden brown and topped with a tangy horseradish sauce. Steamed parslied potatoes and cabbage salad are traditional partners for the *schnitzel*.

Menu 3 is a dramatic meal that provides each person with a whole baked fish stuffed with a nut and bread-crumb filling. Marinated cauliflower and bell pepper salad makes a light and refreshing counterpoint to the fish.

Simple flowers and dinnerware suit this easy Hungarian meal of skewered vegetables and meat, radish salad, and baked Brussels sprouts topped with sour cream.

Brigand's Brochettes
Baked Brussels Sprouts
Radish Salad

The baked Brussels sprouts casserole is very simple to assemble and would be equally good made with cauliflower, turnips, or new potatoes—or a mixture of these vegetables. Brussels sprouts resemble tiny cabbages and have a delicate cabbage flavor. Buy compact, bright green sprouts; avoid any that are wilted or yellowing.

For the brochettes, select vegetables of roughly uniform size. The new potatoes, onions, and mushroom caps should be about 1½ inches in diameter.

WHAT TO DRINK

A full-bodied white wine, such as a good-quality California Chardonnay, would be fine here. For authenticity, serve the Hungarian Egri Bikavér.

SHOPPING LIST AND STAPLES

1¾ pounds hot Italian link sausages
½ pound slab bacon, sliced ½ inch thick (about 3 slices)
2 pounds Brussels sprouts (about 24 medium-size sprouts)
1½ pounds red radishes
6 or 7 small new potatoes (about ¾ pound total weight)
3 medium-size red bell peppers (about 1 pound total weight)
16 medium-size mushrooms (about 1 pound total weight)
Small head curly leaf lettuce
5 small onions (about 1½ pounds total weight)
Small bunch chives
Large lemon
½ pint sour cream
2½ tablespoons unsalted butter
2 quarts vegetable oil (optional)
1¼ cups good-quality olive oil
1 loaf unsliced firm-textured brown or white bread (optional)
½ cup unseasoned dry bread crumbs
Salt and freshly ground pepper

UTENSILS

Food processor (optional)
Large deep heavy-gauge skillet (optional)
2 large saucepans, 1 with cover
Small saucepan
Collapsible vegetable steamer
Broiler pan with rack
Medium-size ovenproof casserole
Jelly-roll pan or large platter
Medium-size bowl
Colander
Measuring cups and spoons
Chef's knife
Paring knife
Bread knife (optional)
Basting brush
Metal tongs
Small jar with tight-fitting lid
Eight 12-inch skewers, preferably metal
Deep-fat thermometer (optional)

START-TO-FINISH STEPS

The Day Before or the Morning of Serving
1. Follow brochettes recipe steps 1 through 5.
2. While potatoes are cooling, follow Brussels sprouts recipe steps 1 through 3.
3. While Brussels sprouts are cooking, follow brochettes recipe steps 6 and 7.
4. Follow Brussels sprouts recipe steps 4 and 5, and brochettes recipe steps 8 and 9 if desired.
5. Follow salad recipe steps 1 and 2.

Thirty Minutes Before Serving
1. Follow Brussels sprouts recipe step 6 and salad recipe step 3.
2. Follow brochettes recipe step 10.
3. While brochettes are broiling, follow salad recipe step 4.
4. Follow brochettes recipe step 11 and Brussels sprouts recipe step 7. (If using combination oven-broiler, place casserole on lower rack.)
5. While brochettes and Brussels sprouts are cooking, follow salad recipe step 5.
6. Follow brochettes recipe step 12, Brussels sprouts recipe step 8, and serve with salad.

RECIPES

Brigand's Brochettes

6 or 7 small new potatoes (about ¾ pound total weight)
1¾ pounds hot Italian link sausage

½ pound slab bacon, sliced ½ inch thick (about 3 slices)
5 small onions (about 1½ pounds total weight)
3 medium-size red bell peppers (about 1 pound
    total weight)
16 medium-size mushrooms (about 1 pound total weight)
Salt and freshly ground pepper
1 cup olive oil
2 quarts vegetable oil (optional)
1 loaf unsliced firm-textured brown or white bread
    (optional)

1. Bring 1 quart water to a boil in large saucepan over high heat.
2. Meanwhile, scrub potatoes. Cut sausage crosswise into ¾-inch pieces. Cut bacon into 1-inch pieces. Set aside.
3. Add potatoes to boiling water and cook over medium heat 15 minutes, or until almost cooked through.
4. Meanwhile, peel onions and cut into ¼-inch-thick slices. Wash bell peppers and dry with paper towels. Halve, core, and seed peppers, and cut into 1-inch squares. Wipe mushrooms clean with damp paper towels. Remove stems and reserve for another use. Set mushroom caps aside.
5. Turn potatoes into colander to drain and cool slightly.
6. Cut potatoes into ½-inch-thick slices. Thread eight 12-inch skewers as follows: Start with mushroom cap and alternate pieces of potato, sausage, bell pepper, bacon, and onion in any order you like. (Leave about 2 inches of skewer free if using bread.) Finish each skewer with a mushroom cap. Season brochettes with salt and pepper.
7. Place brochettes in jelly-roll pan or on large platter, in 2 layers if necessary. Pour olive oil over brochettes and turn each to coat with oil. Cover pan with plastic wrap and refrigerate until 20 minutes before serving.
8. If using bread, heat 2 quarts vegetable oil in large, deep heavy-gauge skillet until temperature of oil registers 350 to 400 degrees on deep-fat thermometer. (You should keep temperature within this range while frying.)
9. Meanwhile, line large plate with double thickness of paper towels. Trim bread loaf to measure 8 by 3 by 3 inches; cut loaf into eight 1-inch-thick slices. Cut shallow notch in one side of each slice. Working in batches if necessary, deep fry bread in hot oil, turning once, about 2 minutes, or until crisp. Using tongs, transfer fried bread to paper-towel-lined plate and when cool cover loosely with plastic wrap until needed.
10. Twenty minutes before serving, preheat broiler. Turn brochettes to coat with olive oil and arrange on rack in broiler pan. Broil 4 inches from heat 10 minutes. Reserve olive oil for basting.
11. Turn brochettes, baste with reserved olive oil, and broil another 10 minutes, or until meat and vegetables are browned.
12. To serve, place 2 fried bread slices, if using, notched-side up, on opposite sides of 4 dinner plates. Balance a skewer between each pair of bread slices. Spoon pan juices over bread and brochettes and serve. Place remaining brochettes on platter, cover with aluminum foil, and keep warm on stovetop.

Baked Brussels Sprouts

2 pounds Brussels sprouts (about 24 medium-size
    sprouts)
2½ tablespoons unsalted butter
Salt
Freshly ground pepper
¾ cup sour cream
½ cup unseasoned dry bread crumbs

1. In large saucepan fitted with vegetable steamer, bring about 1 inch water to a boil over high heat.
2. Meanwhile, wash and trim Brussels sprouts.
3. Place sprouts in steamer, cover pan, and cook 10 minutes.
4. Drain sprouts and turn into medium-size ovenproof casserole.
5. Melt butter in small saucepan over medium heat. Pour butter over sprouts and season with salt and pepper to taste. Cover casserole with plastic wrap and refrigerate until 30 minutes before serving.
6. Thirty minutes before serving, uncover casserole and set out to come to room temperature.
7. Ten minutes before serving, spoon sour cream evenly over sprouts and sprinkle with bread crumbs. Bake sprouts in 500-degree oven until heated through.
8. Serve sprouts directly from casserole or spoon sprouts and topping carefully onto serving platter.

Radish Salad

1½ pounds red radishes
Small bunch chives
Small head curly leaf lettuce
Large lemon
¼ cup olive oil
Salt
Freshly ground pepper

1. Wash and dry radishes and chives. Trim radishes. Wrap radishes and chives tightly in plastic wrap and refrigerate until needed. Wash lettuce and dry with paper towels. Discard any bruised or discolored leaves. Wrap lettuce in paper towels, enclose in plastic bag, and refrigerate until needed.
2. Halve lemon and squeeze enough juice to measure 3 tablespoons. Combine lemon juice, olive oil, and salt and pepper to taste in small jar with tight-fitting lid and shake until combined. Refrigerate dressing until 30 minutes before serving.
3. Thirty minutes before serving, set out dressing to come to room temperature.
4. In food processor fitted with slicing disk, or with paring knife, cut radishes into thin slices. Cut chives into ½-inch pieces. Combine radishes and chives in medium-size bowl. Shake dressing to recombine and pour over salad; toss to coat well.
5. To serve, divide lettuce leaves among 4 dinner plates and top with salad.

Fish Schnitzel
Steamed Parslied Potatoes
Red and Green Cabbage Salad

An extremely versatile main dish, the fish *Schnitzel* (which resemble croquettes) can be made with almost any variety of fresh fish. The patties benefit from standing in the refrigerator: The chilling time sets the breading and helps it adhere to the fish.

WHAT TO DRINK

An ideal wine with this meal would be a lightly chilled dry, aromatic Gewürztraminer of medium body. Try one from Alsace, California, or the Pacific Northwest.

Fried fish patties topped with horseradish sauce are delicious with red and green cabbage salad and steamed potatoes sprinkled with chopped parsley.

SHOPPING LIST AND STAPLES

1½ pounds white-fleshed fish fillets, such as flounder, cod, haddock, or whiting
Small head red cabbage (about 1 pound)
Small head green cabbage (about 1 pound)
1½ pounds new potatoes
Small onion
Small bunch scallions
Small bunch parsley
Large lemon
6 eggs
½ cup milk
½ pint sour cream
5 tablespoons unsalted butter

4-ounce jar prepared horseradish with beets
1 cup vegetable oil
½ cup red wine vinegar
2 slices firm home-style white bread
1 cup unseasoned dry bread crumbs
1 cup all-purpose flour
1 tablespoon sugar
1 teaspoon caraway seeds
Salt
Freshly ground pepper

UTENSILS

Food processor or blender
Large heavy-gauge skillet or 2 medium-size skillets
Small skillet
2 large saucepans, 1 with cover
Collapsible vegetable steamer
Jelly-roll pan or baking sheet
Wire rack to fit jelly-roll pan
2 large bowls, 1 nonaluminum
2 small bowls
3 shallow bowls
Colander
Measuring cups and spoons
Chef's knife

Paring knife
2 wooden spoons
Metal spatula
Vegetable peeler (optional)

START-TO-FINISH STEPS

The Day Before or the Morning of Serving
1. Follow schnitzel recipe steps 1 through 8.
2. Follow potatoes recipe step 1.
3. Follow salad recipe steps 1 through 5.

Twenty Minutes Before Serving
1. Follow potatoes recipe steps 2 and 3.
2. While potatoes are cooking, follow schnitzel recipe steps 9 and 10.
3. Follow salad recipe step 6, schnitzel recipe step 11, potatoes recipe step 4, and serve.

RECIPES

Fish Schnitzel

2 slices firm home-style white bread
½ cup milk
6 eggs

Small onion
5 tablespoons unsalted butter
1½ pounds white-fleshed fish fillets, such as flounder,
    cod, haddock, or whiting
Salt and freshly ground pepper
1 cup all-purpose flour
1 cup unseasoned dry bread crumbs
½ cup sour cream
1½ tablespoons prepared horseradish with beets
1 cup vegetable oil
Large lemon

1. Place bread in small bowl and pour in milk. Set bread aside to soak 5 minutes.
2. Meanwhile, separate 3 eggs, placing yolks in shallow bowl and reserving whites for another use. Peel onion and finely chop enough to measure ½ cup; set aside.
3. Drain off milk and squeeze bread almost dry; set aside.
4. Melt 2 tablespoons butter in small skillet over medium heat. Add onion and sauté, stirring occasionally, about 4 minutes, or until just translucent.
5. Wipe fish fillets with damp paper towels. Cut fillets into large pieces and place in food processor or blender. (If using blender, process in small batches.) Add bread, egg yolks, and onion, and season with salt and pepper. Process, a few seconds at a time, until mixture is coarsely chopped and thoroughly blended. Do not purée.
6. Break remaining 3 eggs into shallow bowl and beat with fork until well blended. Place flour and bread crumbs in separate shallow bowls. Line up bowls with flour first, then eggs, then bread crumbs.
7. Divide fish mixture into 8 equal portions. Shape each portion into an oval patty about ¾ inch thick. One at a time, dredge patties in flour, turning to coat both sides. Pat gently to remove excess. Dip patties into beaten eggs to coat completely, then press into bread crumbs, turning to coat completely. Place each breaded schnitzel on wire rack set in jelly-roll pan or on baking sheet. Cover pan and refrigerate until 10 minutes before serving.
8. In small bowl, stir together sour cream and horseradish. Cover bowl and refrigerate until needed.
9. Ten minutes before serving, heat remaining 3 tablespoons butter with oil in 1 large or 2 medium-size heavy-gauge skillets over medium-high heat. When fat is hot but not smoking, add schnitzels in single layer and fry about 8 minutes, turning once. Reduce heat, if necessary, so they do not brown too quickly.

10. Meanwhile, wash and dry lemon and cut one half into 4 wedges. Reserve remaining half for another use.
11. Divide schnitzels among 4 dinner plates and top each serving with a generous tablespoonful of horseradish sauce and a lemon wedge.

Steamed Parslied Potatoes

1½ pounds new potatoes
Small bunch parsley
Salt

1. Peel potatoes; halve or quarter, depending on size. Place potatoes in large bowl of cold water; cover and refrigerate until needed.
2. Twenty minutes before serving, in large saucepan fitted with vegetable steamer, bring about 1 inch water to a boil over high heat. Drain potatoes, place in steamer, and cook, covered, 15 minutes, or until tender.
3. Meanwhile, wash and dry parsley. Trim ends and discard. Finely chop enough parsley to measure ½ cup.
4. Divide potatoes among 4 dinner plates, or place in serving bowl, and sprinkle with parsley and salt.

Red and Green Cabbage Salad

Small head red cabbage (about 1 pound)
Small head green cabbage (about 1 pound)
1 or 2 scallions
½ cup red wine vinegar
1 tablespoon sugar
1 teaspoon salt
1 teaspoon caraway seeds

1. Bring 1½ quarts water to a boil in large saucepan over high heat.
2. Meanwhile, halve and core cabbages. Thinly slice enough red and green cabbage to measure 4 cups each.
3. Drop sliced cabbage into boiling water and blanch 1 minute. Turn cabbage into colander to drain.
4. Meanwhile, trim scallions and coarsely chop enough to measure 1 tablespoon. In food processor or blender, combine scallions, vinegar, sugar, and salt. Process about 20 seconds, or until ingredients are thoroughly mixed.
5. Transfer cabbage to large nonaluminum bowl. Pour dressing over cabbage, sprinkle with caraway seeds, and toss to combine. Cover bowl with plastic wrap and refrigerate until just before serving, stirring 3 or 4 times.
6. To serve, toss cabbage and divide among 4 plates.

Baked Fish with Pecan Stuffing
Cauliflower, Bell Pepper, and Olive Salad

Whole baked stuffed fish with a salad of cauliflower, bell peppers, and olives is an impressive meal for company.

In Hungary, a cook preparing the fish recipe would use the firm-fleshed white fish called *fogas*, or its smaller relative, *süllő*, which taste like a cross between pike and perch. Since *fogas* and *süllő* are not available in this country, try red snapper, pike, perch, trout, sea bass, or whiting.

WHAT TO DRINK

The cook suggests a red or white wine spritzer (wine mixed with club soda) as both an aperitif and an accompaniment to the meal. A simple dry white wine, such as a Soave or Orvieto from Italy, or a dry Chenin Blanc from California, would be a good match for these dishes.

SHOPPING LIST AND STAPLES

4 whole small red snapper or other firm-fleshed fish (about ¾ pound each), cleaned and boned, with heads and tails intact
Large head cauliflower (about 2 pounds)
Small red bell pepper
Small green bell pepper
Small yellow bell pepper
Small bunch red radishes (optional)
Large head romaine lettuce
Small bunch parsley
2 eggs
2 cups milk
2 tablespoons unsalted butter
7¼-ounce can extra-large pitted black olives
2-ounce tin flat anchovy fillets, or 2 teaspoons anchovy paste
¾ cup good-quality olive oil
1 tablespoon red or white wine vinegar
2 teaspoons Dijon mustard
10 slices firm home-style white bread
3-ounce package whole pecans or walnuts
Salt
Freshly ground pepper

UTENSILS

Food processor (optional)
Blender
Large saucepan with cover
Collapsible vegetable steamer
Jelly-roll pan
Large nonaluminum bowl
Medium-size bowl
Small bowl
Colander
Large strainer
Salad spinner (optional)
Measuring cups and spoons
Chef's knife
Paring knife

Wide metal spatula
Basting brush

START-TO-FINISH STEPS

The Day Before Serving
1. Wash and dry parsley. Set aside 4 sprigs for garnish and chop enough remaining parsley to measure 3 tablespoons for fish recipe and 1 tablespoon for salad recipe.
2. Follow fish recipe steps 1 through 6.
3. Follow salad recipe steps 1 through 8.

Thirty Minutes Before Serving
1. Follow fish recipe step 7 and salad recipe step 9.
2. Follow fish recipe step 8.
3. While fish is baking, follow salad recipe steps 10 and 11.
4. Follow fish recipe step 9 and serve with salad.

RECIPES

Baked Fish with Pecan Stuffing

10 slices firm home-style white bread
2 cups milk
2 eggs
½ cup whole pecans or walnuts
3 tablespoons chopped parsley, plus 4 sprigs for garnish
Salt
Freshly ground pepper
4 whole small red snapper or other firm-fleshed fish (about ¾ pound each), cleaned and boned, with heads and tails intact
4 tablespoons good-quality olive oil
2 tablespoons unsalted butter, well chilled
1 red radish for garnish (optional)

1. Place bread in medium-size bowl and pour in milk. Let bread soak 5 minutes.
2. Meanwhile, separate eggs, dropping yolks into container of food processor or blender and reserving whites for another use.
3. Drain bread and squeeze almost dry.
4. For stuffing, add bread, pecans or walnuts, chopped parsley, and salt and pepper to taste to egg yolks in food processor or blender. Process, turning machine on and off, no more than 15 seconds; nuts should not be too finely ground.
5. Rinse fish and pat dry with paper towels. Fill cavity of each fish with about ½ cup stuffing; do not overfill, as stuffing will expand during baking. (Wrap any extra stuffing in foil to bake along with fish.) As each fish is stuffed, place in jelly-roll pan. Pour 1 tablespoon olive oil over each fish; using your hands, rub oil over skin of each fish to coat completely. Cover pan with plastic wrap and refrigerate until 30 minutes before serving.
6. Cut butter into ¼-inch squares; wrap and refrigerate until 30 minutes before serving.
7. Thirty minutes before serving, preheat oven to 400

degrees. Wash and trim radish, if using, and cut into thin slices. Halve slices and set aside.

8. Season fish with salt and pepper and top each fish with a few squares of butter. Bake about 25 minutes, basting twice with pan juices, until outer flesh springs back readily when pressed with fingers and inner flesh appears opaque at fleshiest part when fish is pierced with a sharp knife.

9. Using wide metal spatula, transfer a fish to each of 4 dinner plates. Spoon some pan juices over each, and cover each fish eye with a parsley sprig, and some radish slices, if desired.

Cauliflower, Bell Pepper, and Olive Salad

Large head cauliflower (about 2 pounds)
Small red bell pepper
Small green bell pepper
Small yellow bell pepper
10 extra-large pitted black olives
½ cup good-quality olive oil
1 tablespoon chopped parsley
1 tablespoon red or white wine vinegar
2 teaspoons Dijon mustard
2 flat anchovy fillets, or 2 teaspoons anchovy paste
Salt and freshly ground pepper
Large head romaine lettuce

1. In large saucepan fitted with vegetable steamer, bring 1 inch water to a boil over high heat.
2. Meanwhile, wash and trim cauliflower and cut into florets. Place florets in steamer, cover pan, and cook 5 minutes.
3. While cauliflower cooks, wash and dry bell peppers. Halve, core, and seed peppers and cut lengthwise into thin strips; set aside.
4. Lift out steamer, reserving hot water in pan, and turn cauliflower into colander. Refresh under cold running water and set aside to drain.
5. Return water in pan to a boil. Replace steamer and add peppers. Cover pan and cook 1 minute. Meanwhile, drain olives and quarter lengthwise; place in large nonaluminum bowl.
6. Lift out steamer and turn peppers into large strainer; refresh peppers under cold running water and set aside to drain.
7. Meanwhile, for dressing combine olive oil, chopped parsley, vinegar, mustard, anchovies or anchovy paste, and salt and pepper to taste in blender. Blend about 15 seconds, or until emulsified.
8. Add cauliflower and peppers to olives in large nonaluminum bowl. Pour dressing over salad and toss well. Cover bowl with plastic wrap and refrigerate until 30 minutes before serving.
9. Thirty minutes before serving, remove salad from refrigerator. Toss salad and set aside to come to room temperature.
10. Wash romaine and dry in salad spinner or with paper towels. Discard any bruised or discolored leaves.

11. Place 2 or 3 large romaine leaves on each dinner plate and top with salad.

ADDED TOUCH

Hungary is famed for its pastries, and all Hungarian cooks have their own versions of this rich cottage cheese cake, known as *turós pite*. Meringue is piped on top in an appealing lattice pattern. Be sure to wash and dry the beaters and bowl after mixing the pastry dough; any trace of grease or egg yolk will keep the egg whites from beating up properly.

Latticed Cottage Cheese Cake

Pastry:
1¼ cups all-purpose flour
½ teaspoon baking soda
Pinch of salt
4 tablespoons unsalted butter,
    at room temperature
¼ cup sour cream
¼ cup sugar
1 egg, at room temperature

Topping:
1 cup cottage cheese
¼ cup sour cream
¼ cup plus 2 tablespoons sugar
1 egg yolk, at room temperature
1 tablespoon all-purpose flour
1 teaspoon finely grated orange zest
¼ cup golden raisins
2 egg whites, at room temperature

1. Preheat oven to 375 degrees.
2. Prepare pastry: In large bowl, combine flour, baking soda, salt, butter, and sour cream. Beat with electric mixer about 1 minute, or until mixture resembles coarse cornmeal. Add sugar and egg and mix about 15 seconds, or just until dough forms a ball. Press dough into 9-inch square cake pan.
3. Bake pastry 20 minutes. Wash and dry beaters and bowl.
4. While pastry bakes, prepare topping: In food processor, combine cottage cheese, sour cream, ¼ cup sugar, the egg yolk, flour, and orange zest. Process about 15 seconds, or until puréed. With rubber spatula, fold in raisins.
5. Place egg whites in large bowl and beat with electric mixer until frothy. Add remaining 2 tablespoons sugar and continue beating until soft peaks form.
6. After cake has baked 20 minutes, remove pan from oven and pour cottage cheese topping over cake. Fill pastry bag fitted with medium-size round tip with beaten egg whites and pipe meringue over topping in lattice pattern, making 4 strips in each direction. Or, spoon meringue onto topping in lattice pattern.
7. Return cake to oven and bake an additional 15 minutes, or until topping is firm and meringue is browned. Let cake cool to room temperature and cut into squares to serve.

Marilyn Hansen

MENU 1 (Left)
Beef Stroganoff with Kasha
Beets and Oranges Vinaigrette

MENU 2
Bouillabaisse with Croutons and Rouille
Tomato-Chutney Aspic

MENU 3
Swedish Meatballs
Cucumber and Radish Salad

Marilyn Hansen cites her extensive world travels as the major influence on her cooking. Wherever she visits, she makes a point of going to local restaurants and wineries and of collecting recipes from native cooks. When cooking at home, she often streamlines and lightens traditional recipes to save time and to suit diet-conscious friends. In the three menus she presents here, she gives new twists to some classic international recipes.

The highlight of Menu 1 is the Russian favorite beef Stroganoff, sautéed strips or cubes of beef in a rich sour-cream-based sauce. Here Marilyn Hansen reduces calories by substituting low-fat yogurt for some of the sour cream. *Kasha*, or buckwheat groats, and dark pumpernickel bread are served with the Stroganoff.

Bouillabaisse is the main course of Menu 2, an ideal buffet meal. In this prepare-ahead version of the classic French seafood stew, the cook uses several kinds of fish as well as shrimp and mussels. For an original touch, she adds curry powder instead of the usual saffron threads. Tomato aspic, flavored with lemon juice and chutney and presented on a bed of watercress, is the salad.

In the Scandinavian-inspired Menu 3, Marilyn Hansen gives traditional Swedish meatballs new zest with allspice and caraway seeds. She cooks the meatballs in advance, then reheats them in a creamy but not overly heavy gravy before serving. Marinated cucumbers with sliced radishes and radish sprouts are the colorful complement.

Everyone will welcome this substantial cold-weather dinner of beef Stroganoff served with kasha *and buttered black bread. The light salad of beets and oranges is sprinkled with pine nuts.*

Beef Stroganoff with Kasha
Beets and Oranges Vinaigrette

For a more dramatic presentation, serve the beef Stroganoff in a bread "tureen." Select a dense 1-pound round loaf of dark pumpernickel bread and, using a serrated knife, cut off a lid about 2 inches from the top of the loaf. With a spoon, scoop out the interior of the loaf to form a bowl, leaving the walls about ¾ to 1 inch thick. Wrap the bowl and its lid in a plastic bag until serving time. Just before serving, place the bowl and lid on a cookie sheet in a preheated 350-degree oven to warm for 10 minutes. Spoon the *kasha* onto a large platter. Place the bread tureen on the bed of *kasha* and fill it with Stroganoff. To serve, spoon the Stroganoff onto individual dinner plates and cut the bread into wedges.

WHAT TO DRINK

The cook suggests a robust wine to match the earthy flavors of this menu. A California Zinfandel, Cabernet Sauvignon, or Merlot would be equally good.

SHOPPING LIST AND STAPLES

1½ pounds boneless top sirloin steak cut 1 inch thick, or flank steak
6 medium-size fresh beets (about 1 pound total weight)
½ pound white mushrooms
Large head Bibb lettuce or large bunch watercress
Small bunch scallions
Medium-size onion
Medium-size clove garlic
Small bunch each dill and parsley
2 medium-size navel oranges or blood oranges
1 egg
1 pint sour cream
½ pint low-fat yogurt
1 stick unsalted butter, approximately
¼ pound chèvre
3 cups beef stock, preferably homemade, or canned
6-ounce can pitted black olives
½ cup vegetable oil, approximately
3 tablespoons white wine vinegar
1 tablespoon Worcestershire sauce
1 teaspoon Dijon mustard
2 teaspoons honey
2-ounce jar capers
Large loaf dark pumpernickel bread
13-ounce package medium or coarse kasha

2-ounce jar pine nuts
Salt and freshly ground black pepper

UTENSILS

Large deep heavy-gauge skillet
Small skillet
Large heavy-gauge saucepan with cover
Medium-size saucepan
Collapsible vegetable steamer
Medium-size bowl
Colander
Strainer
Measuring cups and spoons
Chef's knife
Paring knife
2 wooden spoons
Slotted spatula
Small jar with tight-fitting lid

START-TO-FINISH STEPS

The Day Before or the Morning of Serving

1. Follow Stroganoff recipe steps 1 and 2 and salad recipe steps 1 through 5.
2. Follow Stroganoff recipe steps 3 through 6.

Fifteen Minutes Before Serving

1. Follow kasha recipe steps 1 through 3 and Stroganoff recipe steps 7 and 8.
2. While kasha and Stroganoff are cooking, follow salad recipe step 6.
3. Follow kasha recipe steps 4 and 5.
4. Follow Stroganoff recipe steps 9 and 10 and serve with salad.

RECIPES

Beef Stroganoff with Kasha

1½ pounds boneless top sirloin steak cut 1 inch thick, or flank steak
Medium-size onion
Small bunch scallions
Medium-size clove garlic
½ pound white mushrooms
Small bunch dill

¼ cup capers
6-ounce can pitted black olives
6 tablespoons unsalted butter, approximately
2 tablespoons vegetable oil
2 cups sour cream
1 cup low-fat yogurt
1½ teaspoons salt
½ teaspoon freshly ground black pepper
1 tablespoon Worcestershire sauce
¼ pound chèvre
Large loaf dark pumpernickel bread
Kasha (see following recipe)

1. Wrap beef in plastic or foil and place in freezer at least 30 minutes, or until partially frozen.
2. Meanwhile, peel onion and halve lengthwise. Cut into thin wedges; set aside. Wash, dry, and trim scallions. Cut enough scallions, including green tops, diagonally into ½-inch-thick slices to measure about ⅔ cup. Peel and crush garlic. Wipe mushrooms clean with damp paper towels and slice thinly. Wash dill and pat dry. Wrap and refrigerate 4 sprigs for garnish and finely chop enough remaining dill to measure ½ cup. Drain capers. Drain olives and thinly slice enough to measure ½ cup.
3. When beef is firm, cut across grain into thin slices. Cut slices into ½-inch-wide by 2-inch-long strips.
4. In large deep heavy-gauge skillet, melt 1 tablespoon butter in 1 tablespoon oil over medium-high heat. Add one third of beef strips and sauté, stirring, about 2 minutes, or until browned. Using slotted spatula, transfer cooked beef to medium-size bowl. Sauté remaining beef in two batches and add to bowl.
5. Add onion to skillet and sauté, stirring, 2 minutes, or until slightly wilted; add to bowl with beef. Add remaining 1 tablespoon oil and 1 tablespoon butter to skillet along with scallions, garlic, and mushrooms, and sauté, stirring, 1 minute; add to beef.
6. Add sour cream, yogurt, chopped dill, salt, and pepper to skillet and cook, stirring, 2 minutes, or until almost boiling. (Do not allow mixture to boil.) Add Worcestershire sauce, capers, olives, and beef-onion mixture, and stir to blend. Return mixture to bowl, cover, and refrigerate until about 15 minutes before serving.
7. About 15 minutes before serving, turn Stroganoff into large heavy-gauge skillet and cook, stirring occasionally, 7 to 10 minutes, or until heated through. Do not allow Stroganoff to boil.
8. Meanwhile, cut chèvre into small cubes; set aside. Slice bread, and butter generously.
9. When Stroganoff is hot, stir in chèvre and mix gently; chèvre does not have to melt completely.
10. To serve, divide kasha among 4 dinner plates. Spoon Stroganoff over kasha and garnish with dill sprigs. Serve with buttered bread.

Kasha

3 cups beef stock
1 cup medium or coarse kasha
1 egg
¾ teaspoon salt
¼ teaspoon freshly ground black pepper
Small bunch parsley
2 tablespoons unsalted butter

1. In medium-size saucepan, bring beef stock to a boil over high heat.
2. Meanwhile, combine kasha, egg, salt, and pepper in large heavy-gauge saucepan over low heat. Mix well and stir until kasha is dry.
3. When stock boils, add it to kasha mixture and cover pan. Reduce heat to medium-low and cook, stirring with fork once or twice, 7 to 10 minutes, or until kasha grains are tender.
4. Wash and dry parsley. Finely chop enough parsley to measure ¼ cup.
5. Add parsley and butter to kasha, tossing with fork to combine. Cover and keep warm on stove top until ready to serve.

Beets and Oranges Vinaigrette

6 medium-size fresh beets (about 1 pound total weight)
2 medium-size navel oranges or blood oranges
½ cup pine nuts
⅓ cup vegetable oil
3 tablespoons white wine vinegar
2 teaspoons honey
1 teaspoon Dijon mustard
¼ teaspoon salt
¼ teaspoon freshly ground pepper
Large head Bibb lettuce or large bunch watercress

1. Bring 1 inch of water to a boil in large heavy-gauge saucepan. Meanwhile, wash beets, being careful not to damage skin. Trim beet tops, leaving 1 inch of tops attached. Place beets in vegetable steamer over boiling water, cover pan, and steam 15 to 20 minutes, or until tender.
2. Meanwhile, peel oranges, removing all white pith. Slice oranges crosswise into ¼-inch-thick slices, place in plastic bag, and refrigerate until ready to serve.
3. In small dry skillet, toast pine nuts over medium heat, stirring, about 2 minutes, or until lightly browned. Remove pan from heat; add oil, vinegar, honey, mustard, salt, and pepper, and stir to blend. Pour dressing into jar with tight-fitting lid and refrigerate until needed.
4. When beets are cooked, turn into colander and cool under cold running water; drain well. Slip off skins and cut beets into ¼-inch-thick slices. Place beets in plastic bag and refrigerate until needed.
5. Wash lettuce or watercress and dry in salad spinner or with paper towels. Wrap in dry paper towels, place in plastic bag, and refrigerate until needed.
6. Just before serving, make a bed of lettuce or watercress on each of 4 salad plates. Arrange beet and orange slices on greens. Shake salad dressing well to recombine, and drizzle some dressing over each salad.

Bouillabaisse with Croutons and Rouille
Tomato-Chutney Aspic

French cooks typically use saffron to color and flavor their *bouillabaisse*. Here the cook substitutes curry powder, which is less costly and adds a subtle flavor all its own. If you prefer the more traditional seasoning, use ½ teaspoon saffron threads in place of the curry powder. Let your guests spoon the *rouille* (garlic mayonnaise) over the *bouillabaisse* to suit their individual tastes.

Although it may sound tricky, making an aspic with unflavored gelatin is quite simple. To get the best results, use only one envelope of gelatin; never try for a thicker aspic by adding more gelatin or the aspic will be rubbery. The aspic should be refrigerated until just before serving, and, if served as part of a buffet, should be presented on a chilled platter.

WHAT TO DRINK

This meal demands a crisp, well-chilled white wine. Try an Italian Pinot Grigio or Verdicchio.

SHOPPING LIST AND STAPLES

½ pound flounder or sole fillets
½ pound catfish, yellow perch, or freshwater trout fillets, or salmon or cod steaks
1 pound medium-size shrimp
½ pound mussels (about 12)
Medium-size leek
Small fennel bulb
Small bunch celery with leaves
Large bunch watercress
1 medium-size plus 1 small onion
3 medium-size cloves garlic
Small bunch fresh thyme, or ½ teaspoon dried
Small bunch fresh parsley
2 medium-size lemons
½ pint sour cream
½ pint low-fat yogurt
35-ounce can Italian plum tomatoes
12-ounce can tomato juice
7 tablespoons good-quality olive oil
1 cup mayonnaise
Three 8-ounce bottles clam juice
10-ounce jar mango chutney
½ teaspoon Worcestershire sauce
½ teaspoon hot pepper sauce
Large loaf Italian or French bread

Tempting bouillabaisse *with a peppery* rouille *makes an elegant meal at any time of year. Present the rectangles of shimmering tomato aspic with their yogurt-and-sour-cream topping on a bed of crisp watercress.*

8-ounce package chopped walnuts
1 envelope unflavored gelatin
1 bay leaf
1 teaspoon curry powder, or ½ teaspoon saffron threads
1 teaspoon paprika
¼ teaspoon red pepper flakes
Salt
Freshly ground black pepper
½ cup dry white wine or dry vermouth
1 tablespoon Sambuca or other anise-flavored liqueur

UTENSILS

Food processor or blender
Large heavy-gauge nonaluminum stockpot or Dutch
    oven, with cover
2 medium-size nonaluminum saucepans
17 x 11-inch baking sheet
Small loaf pan
Medium-size bowl
3 small bowls
Salad spinner (optional)
Large strainer
Measuring cups and spoons
Chef's knife
Paring knife
2 wooden spoons
Metal spatula
Rubber spatula
Ladle
Stiff-bristled brush

START-TO-FINISH STEPS

The Day Before or the Morning of Serving

1. Peel garlic and mince enough to measure 1 tablespoon for bouillabaisse recipe and 1 tablespoon for rouille recipe. Halve 1 lemon and squeeze enough juice to measure 1 tablespoon each for rouille and aspic recipes.
2. Follow aspic recipe steps 1 through 4.
3. Follow bouillabaisse recipe steps 1 through 8.
4. Follow rouille recipe steps 1 and 2.

Fifteen Minutes Before Serving

1. Follow rouille recipe step 3, bouillabaisse recipe steps 9 through 11, and aspic recipe step 5.
2. Follow bouillabaisse recipe steps 12 through 14 and

aspic recipe step 6.
3. Follow bouillabaisse recipe steps 15 and 16 and serve with aspic.

RECIPES

Bouillabaisse with Croutons and Rouille

1 medium-size plus 1 small onion
Medium-size leek
2 medium-size stalks celery with leaves
Small fennel bulb
5 tablespoons good-quality olive oil
1 tablespoon minced garlic
35-ounce can Italian plum tomatoes
Small bunch fresh thyme, or ½ teaspoon dried
1 teaspoon curry powder, or ½ teaspoon saffron threads
¼ teaspoon red pepper flakes
1 bay leaf
½ cup dry white wine or dry vermouth
2 teaspoons salt
Freshly ground black pepper
1 pound medium-size shrimp
Three 8-ounce bottles clam juice
½ pound flounder or sole fillets
½ pound catfish, yellow perch, or freshwater trout fillets,
    or salmon or cod steaks
½ pound mussels (about 12)
Large loaf Italian or French bread
Small bunch parsley
1 tablespoon Sambuca or other anise-flavored liqueur
Rouille (see following recipe)

1. Peel medium-size onion and finely chop enough to measure 1 cup. Reserve small onion. Trim root end from leek and split leek lengthwise. Wash leek thoroughly under cold running water to remove all grit and dry with paper towel. Discard dark green tops of leek and finely chop enough white and light green parts to measure 1 cup. Wash, dry, and trim celery. Finely chop enough celery stalks and leaves to measure 1 cup. Wash, dry, and trim fennel bulb. Finely chop enough fennel to measure ¾ cup.
2. Heat 3 tablespoons olive oil over medium heat in large heavy-gauge nonaluminum stockpot or Dutch oven. Add chopped onion, leek, celery, fennel, and garlic, and sauté, stirring often, 5 minutes, or until softened.
3. Meanwhile, drain tomatoes in strainer over medium-size bowl; reserve juice. Coarsely chop enough tomatoes

to measure 2 cups. Wash fresh thyme, if using, and dry with paper towels. Strip enough leaves from stems to measure 1 tablespoon.

4. Add tomatoes and their juice, thyme, curry powder, red pepper flakes, bay leaf, wine, salt, and pepper to taste to stockpot. Bring mixture to a boil, reduce heat to medium-low, cover, and simmer 15 minutes.

5. Meanwhile, peel and devein shrimp, *reserving* shells (see page 49). Wrap and refrigerate shrimp until needed.

6. Place clam juice, shrimp shells, and small unpeeled onion in medium-size nonaluminum saucepan, and bring to a boil over high heat. Reduce heat to low and simmer 10 minutes.

7. Meanwhile, cut all fish fillets or steaks into 2 by 1-inch pieces. Scrub mussels with stiff-bristled brush, remove hairlike beards, and rinse mussels under cold running water. Wrap fish and mussels in separate plastic bags and refrigerate until needed.

8. Strain broth, discard shrimp shells and onion, and add broth to tomato mixture. Stir to combine, cover, and refrigerate soup base until needed.

9. Fifteen minutes before serving, preheat oven to 400 degrees.

10. Bring soup base to a boil over medium-high heat.

11. Cut bread into ½-inch-thick slices and arrange in a single layer on 17 by 11-inch baking sheet.

12. Toast bread in oven about 7 minutes, or until lightly browned.

13. Meanwhile, add fish pieces, shrimp, and mussels to boiling soup base, reduce heat to medium-low, and simmer 3 to 4 minutes, or just until fish is opaque, shrimp turn pink, and mussels open.

14. Wash and dry parsley. Finely chop enough to measure 2 tablespoons.

15. Discard any mussels that have not opened. Add parsley, Sambuca, and remaining 2 tablespoons olive oil to soup. Taste, and adjust seasonings if necessary.

16. Ladle bouillabaisse into large tureen and serve with hot croutons and rouille. Let guests spoon rouille into stew or spread on croutons.

Rouille

1 cup mayonnaise
2 tablespoons good-quality olive oil
1 tablespoon lemon juice
1 tablespoon minced garlic
1 teaspoon paprika

½ teaspoon salt
¼ teaspoon hot pepper sauce

1. Combine all ingredients in food processor or blender. Process 5 seconds, or just until blended.

2. Turn rouille into small bowl, cover, and refrigerate until 15 minutes before serving.

3. Fifteen minutes before serving, set out rouille to come to room temperature.

Tomato-Chutney Aspic

1 envelope unflavored gelatin
1½ cups tomato juice
⅓ cup mango chutney
1 tablespoon lemon juice
½ teaspoon Worcestershire sauce
¼ teaspoon hot pepper sauce
¾ cup low-fat yogurt
¼ cup sour cream
¼ teaspoon salt
Freshly ground pepper
Large bunch watercress
Medium-size lemon
¾ cup chopped walnuts

1. In small bowl, sprinkle gelatin over 2 tablespoons tomato juice and set aside to soften, about 5 minutes.

2. Meanwhile, place remaining tomato juice in medium-size nonaluminum saucepan. Add chutney, lemon juice, Worcestershire sauce, and hot pepper sauce. Bring to a boil over high heat. Add softened gelatin, reduce heat to low, and stir about 1 minute, or until gelatin dissolves. Pour mixture into small loaf pan, cover, and refrigerate until set, at least 2 hours.

3. In small bowl, combine yogurt, sour cream, salt, and pepper to taste and stir gently to blend. Cover and refrigerate until needed.

4. Wash watercress and dry in salad spinner or with paper towels. Place in plastic bag and refrigerate until needed.

5. Just before serving, arrange watercress on platter, reserving 4 sprigs for garnish. Wash and dry lemon and cut into thin wedges.

6. Cut aspic into 4 equal portions and use spatula to remove from pan. Place aspic on top of watercress. Spoon a dollop of yogurt mixture on top of each portion of aspic and sprinkle with walnuts. Garnish each with a sprig of watercress, and garnish platter with lemon wedges.

Swedish Meatballs
Cucumber and Radish Salad

Flavorful Swedish meatballs and a refreshing salad of thinly sliced cucumbers and radishes is an easy meal for family or company.

For the best results in preparing the meatballs, follow these tips: Chill the ingredients thoroughly before shaping the balls. Moisten your hands with cold water before rolling the seasoned meat between your palms. Handle the meatballs gently so they will have a light texture. Turn the meatballs once during baking to keep them nicely rounded.

WHAT TO DRINK

A full-bodied imported beer suits this simple Scandinavian dinner. Alternatively, select a full-bodied and flavorful white wine, such as a California Chardonnay or a French Saint-Véran.

SHOPPING LIST AND STAPLES

1 pound lean ground beef
½ pound lean ground pork
2 medium-size cucumbers (about 1 pound total weight), plus large cucumber (optional)
Large bunch red radishes
Small package radish sprouts or small bunch watercress
Medium-size onion

Small bunch each dill and parsley
1 egg
½ cup milk
½ pint half-and-half
3 tablespoons unsalted butter
¾ cup beef stock, preferably homemade, or canned
¾ cup white wine vinegar or rice vinegar
1 teaspoon Worcestershire sauce
2 tablespoons all-purpose flour
3 to 4 slices firm home-style white bread
3 tablespoons sugar
1 teaspoon meat extract paste (optional)
1 teaspoon caraway seeds
½ teaspoon ground allspice
Salt and freshly ground black pepper

UTENSILS

Large deep skillet or flameproof casserole, with cover
Large skillet
Small skillet
Roasting pan
9-inch glass pie plate
Large bowl
2 medium-size bowls, 1 nonaluminum
Small bowl
Measuring cups and spoons
Chef's knife
Paring knife
Wooden spoon
Wire whisk
Grater
Vegetable peeler

START-TO-FINISH STEPS

The Day Before or the Morning of Serving

1. Follow salad recipe steps 1 and 2.
2. Follow meatballs recipe steps 1 through 8.
3. Follow salad recipe steps 3 and 4.

Fifteen Minutes Before Serving

1. Follow meatballs recipe step 9.
2. While meatballs are reheating, follow salad recipe steps 5 through 7.
3. Follow meatballs recipe steps 10 and 11 and serve with salad.

RECIPES

Swedish Meatballs

Meatballs:
Medium-size onion
1 tablespoon unsalted butter
3 to 4 slices firm home-style white bread
½ cup cold milk
1½ teaspoons salt
½ teaspoon freshly ground black pepper
1 teaspoon caraway seeds
½ teaspoon ground allspice
1 egg
1 pound lean ground beef, well chilled
½ pound lean ground pork, well chilled

Gravy:
2 tablespoons unsalted butter
2 tablespoons all-purpose flour
1 cup half-and-half
¾ cup beef stock
1 teaspoon Worcestershire sauce
1 teaspoon meat extract paste (optional)
Salt and freshly ground black pepper
Small bunch parsley for garnish

1. Preheat oven to 400 degrees. Line roasting pan with foil.
2. For meatballs, peel onion and finely chop enough to measure ½ cup. In small skillet, melt butter over medium heat. Add onion and sauté 5 minutes, or until tender.
3. Meanwhile, trim crusts from bread. Using coarse side of grater, grate enough bread to measure 1 cup crumbs. In large bowl, combine onion, bread crumbs, milk, salt, pepper, caraway seeds, allspice, and egg; mix well.
4. Add beef and pork to onion mixture; combine well.
5. Using about a teaspoonful of mixture for each meatball, shape meat with hands into about 40 small meatballs and place in foil-lined roasting pan.
6. Bake meatballs, turning once, 12 to 15 minutes, or until meatballs are cooked through and firm when pressed.
7. Turn meatballs into medium-size bowl, cover, and refrigerate until 15 minutes before serving.
8. For gravy, in large skillet, melt butter over medium heat. Add flour and stir until smooth. Add half-and-half and stock and bring to a boil, whisking constantly. Cook mixture, continuing to whisk, 5 minutes, or until gravy

thickens. Whisk in Worcestershire sauce, meat extract paste if using, and salt and pepper to taste. Pour gravy into small bowl, cover, and refrigerate until 15 minutes before serving.

9. Fifteen minutes before serving, pour gravy into large deep skillet or flameproof casserole. Add meatballs and bring gravy to a boil over medium-high heat. Reduce heat to medium-low, cover, and simmer 10 minutes, or until meatballs are heated through. (If necessary, you may hold meatballs and gravy in covered skillet or casserole in preheated 325-degree oven until ready to serve.)

10. Just before serving, wash and dry parsley. Chop enough parsley to measure 1 teaspoon.

11. Divide meatballs and gravy among 4 dinner plates and sprinkle with chopped parsley.

Cucumber and Radish Salad

2 medium-size cucumbers (about 1 pound total weight), plus 1 large cucumber for garnish (optional)
3 teaspoons salt
Large bunch red radishes
¾ cup white wine vinegar or rice vinegar
3 tablespoons sugar
½ teaspoon freshly ground black pepper
Small package radish sprouts or small bunch watercress
Small bunch dill

1. Peel medium-size cucumbers and cut crosswise into ⅛-inch-thick slices.

2. Place half of cucumber slices in glass pie plate and sprinkle with 1 teaspoon salt. Top with remaining cucumber slices and 1 teaspoon salt. Cover with heavy plate to press out excess water. Set cucumbers aside for 20 to 30 minutes.

3. Trim radishes and cut crosswise into very thin slices. Place in plastic bag and refrigerate until needed.

4. For dressing, in medium-size nonaluminum bowl, combine vinegar, sugar, remaining teaspoon salt, and pepper. Drain cucumbers and add to dressing; cover and refrigerate until needed.

5. Just before serving, wash and dry radish sprouts and dill; chop enough to measure 2 tablespoons each. If using cucumber for garnish, cut into fans (see page 9).

6. Pour off and discard most of dressing. Add radishes, radish sprouts, and dill to cucumbers and mix gently.

7. Divide salad among 4 dinner plates. Garnish each plate with a cucumber fan, if desired.

ADDED TOUCH

This pie is a fitting conclusion to a cold-weather meal. Adjust the amount of maple syrup and the baking time to the sweetness and ripeness of the pears.

Deep-Dish Pear Pie

Pastry:

1½ cups unsifted all-purpose flour
½ teaspoon salt
⅓ cup shortening, well chilled
2 tablespoons unsalted butter, well chilled
¼ cup ice water

Filling:

2½ pounds medium-ripe pears, such as Comice or Anjou
2 tablespoons all-purpose flour
2 tablespoons unsalted butter
½ to 1 cup maple syrup
¼ teaspoon salt
¼ teaspoon freshly grated nutmeg
¼ teaspoon ground cinnamon

Glaze:

1 tablespoon milk
1 tablespoon sugar

1. Preheat oven to 425 degrees.

2. Prepare pastry: In large bowl, combine flour and salt. Using pastry blender or 2 knives, cut in shortening and butter until mixture resembles coarse cornmeal.

3. Sprinkle ice water over mixture and stir with fork until dough forms a ball and pulls away from sides of bowl. Cover and refrigerate while making filling.

4. Prepare filling: Peel, halve, and core pears. Cut crosswise into ½-inch-thick slices and place in large bowl.

5. Blend flour with 1 tablespoon butter and add in bits to pears.

6. Add maple syrup to taste, salt, nutmeg, and cinnamon; stir to mix. Pour filling into deep 9-inch pie pan or 10-inch gratin dish. Dot with remaining 1 tablespoon butter.

7. On floured board, roll out pastry to size of pan plus ½ inch. Cover pears with pastry and turn under overhanging pastry. Flute edge and cut several steam vents in pastry. Brush pastry with milk and sprinkle with sugar.

8. Bake pie on middle rack of oven 30 to 45 minutes, or until crust is golden brown and filling is bubbling. Serve warm.

Margaret Fraser

According to Margaret Fraser, Greek immigrants settling throughout Canada have contributed generously to the cuisine of their adopted homeland. Greek markets attract the uninitiated and curious with lavish displays of such delicacies as grape leaves in brine, barrels of oil-cured olives, bundles of dried herbs, and trays of sugar-dusted pastries. "As a result of this exposure," says Margaret Fraser, "we Canadian cooks are adding more and more Greek dishes to our repertoires." The three menus she presents here are all easily assembled Greek meals.

In Menu 1, a number of popular Greek seasonings flavor the dishes: lemon juice in the *taramosalata* (fish roe dip); garlic and rosemary in the marinade for the lamb kabobs; and oregano in the rice-stuffed tomatoes. You can serve the *taramosalata* as an appetizer, but if you do, the cook suggests that you leave it on the table during the meal to eat with the pita.

The *spanakopita*, or spinach pie, of Menu 2 consists of layers of flaky filo pastry enfolding a spinach and feta cheese filling. Although it may appear difficult to make, the pie can be prepared quickly once you master handling the filo dough. As accompaniments, Margaret Fraser serves a chilled version of the lemon soup known in Greece as *avgolemono*, and a salad of marinated artichokes and olives.

Originally a Middle Eastern dish, the *moussaka* of Menu 3 was long ago adopted by the Greeks. This hearty eggplant and ground lamb casserole goes well with a simple romaine salad. Melon balls with *ouzo* cream are the light dessert.

Casual ceramics suit this bright Greek meal of taramosalata with crudités and toasted pita triangles, broiled lamb kabobs, and tomatoes filled with herbed rice.

34

Taramosalata with Crudités and Pita Bread
Lamb Kabobs
Stuffed Tomatoes

The popular Greek appetizer *taramosalata*, known as "poor man's caviar," is a creamy purée most often served as a dip or spread. It is usually made from the tiny orange eggs, or roe (*tarama*), of carp, although occasionally tuna or gray mullet roe is used. Look for *tarama* in bottles in Greek and Middle Eastern markets or in specialty food shops. If you are on a salt-restricted diet, soak the *tarama* in water for 5 to 10 minutes, then drain it well. *Tarama* keeps in the refrigerator for up to three months; *taramosalata* can be made up to five days in advance of serving and stored in the refrigerator.

WHAT TO DRINK

A Cabernet Sauvignon is always a good choice with lamb. Try a young California Cabernet or one from the Médoc region.

SHOPPING LIST AND STAPLES

1¾ pounds lean boneless lamb, cut into 1-inch cubes
4 medium-size tomatoes (about 1½ pounds total weight)
Large red bell pepper
Large zucchini
Small onion
5 medium-size cloves garlic
Small bunch fresh rosemary, or 2 teaspoons dried
Small bunch fresh chives (optional)
3 lemons
10-ounce jar tarama
1¼ cups good-quality olive oil, approximately
⅓ cup long-grain white rice
Two 6-inch pita breads
3 thick slices home-style white bread
2-ounce jar pine nuts
¼ teaspoon dried thyme
¼ teaspoon dried oregano
Salt
Freshly ground pepper

UTENSILS

Food processor or blender
Small skillet
Small saucepan with cover
Shallow 1-quart baking dish
Broiler pan
Shallow glass or ceramic dish
Small bowl
Measuring cups and spoons
Chef's knife
Paring knife
Rubber spatula
Citrus juicer (optional)
Basting brush
Four 10- to 12-inch skewers

START-TO-FINISH STEPS

The Day Before or the Morning of Serving
1. Wash 2 lemons and dry with paper towels. Halve lemons. Cut 3 thick slices from one half for kabobs recipe. Squeeze enough juice from remaining halves to measure ¼ cup for taramosalata recipe. Crush and peel 4 cloves garlic for kabobs recipe. Peel and mince remaining clove for stuffed tomatoes recipe.
2. Follow stuffed tomatoes recipe step 1.
3. Follow kabobs recipe steps 1 and 2.
4. Follow stuffed tomatoes recipe steps 2 through 8.
5. While tomatoes are baking, follow taramosalata recipe steps 1 through 4.

Thirty Minutes Before Serving
1. Follow kabobs recipe step 3, stuffed tomatoes recipe step 9, and taramosalata recipe step 5.
2. Follow kabobs recipe steps 4 through 6.
3. While kabobs are broiling, follow taramosalata recipe steps 6 through 9.
4. Follow stuffed tomatoes recipe step 10, kabobs recipe step 7, and serve with taramosalata.

RECIPES

Taramosalata with Crudités and Pita Bread

3 thick slices home-style white bread
Small onion
½ cup tarama
¼ cup lemon juice
½ teaspoon salt
Freshly ground pepper
½ cup good-quality olive oil
Large zucchini

Large red bell pepper
Two 6-inch pita breads

1. Place white bread on plate, pour ¾ cup water over bread, and let soak 10 minutes.
2. Meanwhile, peel and coarsely chop onion. In food processor or blender, combine onion, tarama, lemon juice, salt, and pepper to taste. Process until combined.
3. Gently squeeze out excess water from bread and tear bread into chunks. Add to food processor or blender and process until smooth.
4. With machine running, add olive oil in a slow, steady stream. Process until mixture is smooth and light pink in color. Transfer to small serving bowl, cover, and refrigerate until 30 minutes before serving.
5. Thirty minutes before serving, set out taramosalata to come to room temperature.
6. Wash zucchini and bell pepper and dry with paper towels. Trim zucchini and cut crosswise into ¼-inch-thick slices. Core and seed bell pepper; cut into 1-inch squares.
7. Cut each pita bread into 6 wedges.
8. Five minutes before serving, wrap pita wedges in foil and warm in broiler or 500-degree oven 2 to 3 minutes. Place in napkin-lined basket to keep warm.
9. Divide zucchini slices and bell pepper squares among 4 salad plates and serve with taramosalata and pita.

Lamb Kabobs

Small bunch fresh rosemary, or 2 teaspoons dried
3 thick slices lemon, plus 1 lemon for garnish
4 medium-size cloves garlic, crushed and peeled
½ cup good-quality olive oil
Salt and freshly ground pepper
1¾ pounds lean boneless lamb, cut into 1-inch cubes

1. Wash fresh rosemary, if using, and pat dry with paper towels. Reserve 4 sprigs for garnish. Mince enough remaining rosemary to measure 2 tablespoons.
2. Combine lemon slices, fresh or dried rosemary, garlic, olive oil, and salt and pepper to taste in shallow glass or ceramic dish. Add lamb, cover with plastic wrap, and refrigerate, turning lamb occasionally, at least 2 hours or overnight.
3. Thirty minutes before serving, preheat broiler. Remove lamb from refrigerator.
4. Wash and dry lemon for garnish. Cut into 12 wedges; set aside.

5. Remove lamb from marinade and thread onto four 10- to 12-inch skewers. Arrange skewers in broiler pan.
6. Broil kabobs about 6 inches from heat, turning occasionally and brushing generously with marinade, 12 minutes, or until browned.
7. Transfer kabobs to dinner plates and garnish with lemon wedges, and rosemary sprigs if desired.

Stuffed Tomatoes

4 medium-size tomatoes (about 1½ pounds total weight)
Salt
⅓ cup long-grain white rice
2 tablespoons pine nuts
2 tablespoons good-quality olive oil
Medium-size clove garlic, minced
¼ teaspoon dried thyme
¼ teaspoon dried oregano
Small bunch chives for garnish (optional)

1. Preheat oven to 375 degrees. Lightly grease shallow 1-quart baking dish.
2. Bring ¾ cup water to a boil over high heat in small saucepan.
3. Wash tomatoes and dry with paper towels. Cut tops off tomatoes. Scoop out and reserve pulp; remove and discard seeds. Lightly salt insides of tomato shells and invert on paper towels to drain.
4. Add rice to boiling water; cover, and cook over medium-low heat 20 minutes, or until tender.
5. Meanwhile, brown pine nuts in small dry skillet over medium heat 3 to 4 minutes, stirring constantly. Transfer pine nuts to small bowl and set aside.
6. Heat oil in skillet over medium heat until hot. Add garlic, thyme, oregano, and reserved tomato pulp and cook 3 to 4 minutes, or until excess liquid has evaporated. Remove skillet from heat and stir in rice and pine nuts.
7. Place tomato shells in prepared baking dish and spoon stuffing into shells.
8. Bake tomatoes 15 to 20 minutes, or until stuffing is lightly browned. Let tomatoes cool slightly, then cover and refrigerate until 30 minutes before serving.
9. Thirty minutes before serving, remove tomatoes from refrigerator to come to room temperature. Wash chives, if using, and dry with paper towels. Mince enough chives to measure 1 tablespoon; reserve remainder for another use.
10. Sprinkle tomatoes with chives, if desired, and transfer to dinner plates.

Chilled Avgolemono
Spanakopita
Marinated Artichokes with Greek Olives

Offer the delicate lemon and egg soup before or with the spanakopita *and the salad of marinated artichokes and olives.*

The spinach and feta cheese filling for the *spanakopita* is wrapped in filo, tissue-thin pastry sheets that are sold frozen in half-pound (about 13 sheets) or one-pound boxes. To prevent the sheets from cracking when you separate them, thaw the entire block of frozen filo in the refrigerator overnight. Never refreeze the extra dough or the sheets may stick together; refrigerate it and use it within a week.

Because filo becomes crumbly when overexposed to air, work quickly and have your other ingredients ready before unrolling the dough. Unroll the dough and place eight sheets, unseparated, on a damp kitchen towel covered with plastic wrap; cover the top sheet with another piece of plastic wrap and a second damp towel. Work with one sheet of dough at a time, leaving the rest covered. The butter you brush on the sheets helps to separate the layers and turn the pastry a golden brown as it bakes. But take care—too much butter will make the pastry soggy. If feta cheese is unavailable, substitute a creamy chèvre or plain cream cheese. The flavor of the finished dish will not be as tangy, but it will still be good.

WHAT TO DRINK

A crisp, dry, flavorful white wine, such as a French Sancerre or a Sauvignon Blanc from California or Italy, goes best with these dishes.

SHOPPING LIST AND STAPLES

1 pound spinach
¼ pound fresh mushrooms
8 to 10 fresh baby artichokes (about ¾ pound total weight), or two 14-ounce cans water-packed artichoke hearts
Medium-size onion
Small bunch fresh rosemary, or 1 teaspoon dried
Small bunch fresh dill
Small bunch fresh mint
3 large lemons
5 eggs
7 tablespoons unsalted butter
½ pound feta cheese
½-pound package frozen filo dough
4 cups chicken stock, preferably homemade (see page 10), or canned
½ cup good-quality olive oil
10-ounce jar small Greek olives
⅓ cup long-grain white rice
½ teaspoon dried oregano
½ teaspoon dried thyme
Salt and freshly ground white and black pepper

UTENSILS

Large skillet
Large saucepan with cover
2 medium-size saucepans, one with cover
Small saucepan
8-inch square baking pan
2 large nonaluminum bowls
Small bowl
Colander
Strainer
Measuring cups and spoons
Chef's knife
Paring knife
Wooden spoon
Slotted spoon
Whisk
Pastry brush
Kitchen scissors
Cheesecloth
Kitchen string

START-TO-FINISH STEPS

The Morning of Serving
1. Wash 2 lemons and dry with paper towels. Halve 1 lemon for artichokes recipe. Squeeze enough juice from remaining lemon to measure ⅓ cup and set aside for avgolemono recipe.
2. Follow spanakopita recipe steps 1 and 2.
3. Follow avgolemono recipe steps 1 and 2 and artichokes recipe steps 1 through 3.
4. Follow avgolemono recipe step 3.
5. While rice is cooking, follow artichokes recipe step 4 and spanakopita recipe step 3.
6. Follow avgolemono recipe step 4 and spanakopita recipe step 4.
7. Follow artichokes recipe steps 5 and 6.
8. Follow spanakopita recipe steps 5 through 10.

About Thirty Minutes Before Serving
1. Follow spanakopita recipe steps 11 and 12.
2. Toward end of spanakopita baking time, follow artichokes recipe steps 7 and 8 and avgolemono recipe steps 5 and 6.
3. Follow spanakopita recipe step 13 and serve with avgolemono and artichokes.

RECIPES

Chilled Avgolemono

4 cups chicken stock
Small bunch mint
⅓ cup long-grain white rice
2 eggs
⅓ cup lemon juice
Salt and freshly ground white pepper
Large lemon for garnish

1. Bring stock to a boil in medium-size saucepan over high heat.
2. Meanwhile, wash mint and pat dry with paper towels. Enclose 4 sprigs mint in small square of cheesecloth and

tie securely with kitchen string. Wrap remaining mint in plastic and reserve.

3. Add cheesecloth packet and rice to stock. Reduce heat to medium-low, cover, and cook 15 to 20 minutes, or until rice is tender. Discard cheesecloth packet.

4. In large nonaluminum bowl, beat eggs with whisk until light and frothy. Add hot stock and rice very slowly, whisking constantly. (If stock is added too quickly, eggs will curdle.) Stir in lemon juice, and salt and pepper to taste. Cover bowl with plastic wrap and refrigerate until just before serving.

5. Just before serving, wash lemon and dry with paper towel. Cut 4 thin slices for garnish. Finely chop enough reserved mint to measure 1 teaspoon.

6. Divide soup among 4 bowls and garnish each with a lemon slice and some chopped mint.

Spanakopita

Small bunch dill
¼ pound fresh mushrooms
Medium-size onion
1 pound spinach
7 tablespoons unsalted butter
3 eggs
½ pound feta cheese
½ teaspoon each dried oregano and thyme
½ teaspoon salt
8 sheets frozen filo dough, thawed

1. Wash dill and pat dry with paper towels. Finely chop enough dill to measure 2 tablespoons. Wipe mushrooms clean with damp paper towels and chop finely. Peel and finely chop onion.

2. Wash spinach in several changes of cold water. Do not dry. Remove tough stems and discard.

3. Place spinach in large saucepan and cook, covered, over medium-high heat 3 to 5 minutes, or until just wilted. Turn spinach into colander and refresh under cold running water. Drain well, pressing out excess moisture with back of spoon. Finely chop spinach; set aside.

4. Melt 2 tablespoons butter in large skillet over medium heat. Add onion and mushrooms and cook 3 minutes, or until soft. Remove from heat and add spinach; stir to combine and allow to cool 10 minutes.

5. Beat eggs lightly in small bowl and add to spinach mixture. Crumble in feta and add chopped dill, oregano, thyme, and salt. Set aside.

6. Melt remaining 5 tablespoons butter in small saucepan.

7. Butter bottom and sides of 8-inch square baking pan. Brush 1 sheet of filo lightly on one side with melted butter. Fold sheet to 8-inch width so that when placed in pan it completely covers bottom and overhangs evenly on two opposite sides.

8. Rotate pan a quarter turn and repeat procedure with another sheet of buttered filo. Repeat with 4 more sheets of filo, rotating pan a quarter turn each time. (Filo should hang over edges of pan on all four sides.)

9. Spread spinach-cheese filling over filo, smoothing top.

One side at a time, fold overhanging filo over filling.

10. Cut remaining 2 sheets of filo into four 8-inch squares. Layer squares on top of filled pastry, brushing each square with melted butter before placing the next on top. Score top of spanakopita with sharp paring knife just through pastry layers (dividing it into 4 quarters) to ensure neat portions after baking. Cover with plastic wrap and refrigerate until 30 minutes before serving.

11. About 30 minutes before serving, preheat oven to 375 degrees.

12. Bake spanakopita 30 minutes, or until golden brown.

13. Cut spanakopita into four pieces and transfer to dinner plates.

Marinated Artichokes with Greek Olives

8 to 10 fresh baby artichokes (about ¾ pound total weight),
   or two 14-ounce cans water-packed artichoke hearts
Small bunch fresh rosemary, or 1 teaspoon dried
Large lemon, halved
½ cup good-quality olive oil
Freshly ground black pepper
1 cup small Greek olives

1. Bring 3 cups water to a boil in medium-size saucepan.

2. Meanwhile, wash fresh artichokes and fresh rosemary, if using, and pat dry with paper towels. Roughly chop enough rosemary to measure 1 tablespoon and reserve remaining rosemary for another use. Pull off and discard any discolored leaves from artichokes and trim stems. Using kitchen scissors, cut off tips of remaining leaves and rub cut surfaces with 1 lemon half.

3. If using canned artichokes, rinse and drain in colander, and sprinkle with juice from lemon half, if desired.

4. Add used lemon half and fresh artichokes to boiling water. Cover pan and simmer gently over medium-low heat 15 minutes, or until artichokes are tender when stems are pierced with a fork.

5. Combine olive oil, fresh or dried rosemary, and pepper to taste in large nonaluminum bowl. Cut remaining lemon half into 3 or 4 slices and add to bowl.

6. Drain fresh artichokes in colander and halve lengthwise. Add fresh or canned artichokes to marinade, cover bowl with plastic wrap, and refrigerate until 30 minutes before serving, stirring occasionally.

7. Just before serving, drain olives in strainer.

8. Using slotted spoon, transfer artichokes to salad plates. Divide olives among plates and serve.

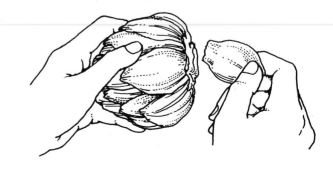

Moussaka
Romaine with Cucumber-Yogurt Dressing
Sesame Pita Crisps/Melon with Ouzo Cream

For an informal buffet serve moussaka *hot from the oven, toasted pita triangles, a green salad, and melon balls with* ouzo *cream.*

The *moussaka*, with its custardy topping, is an excellent make-ahead dish that improves in flavor the longer it stands. Whether you bake it ahead and reheat it or refrigerate the unbaked dish to cook at mealtime, you will get fine results. The eggplants you choose should have smooth, glossy, unblemished skin. They should be firm and feel heavy for their size.

The Greek liqueur *ouzo*, used in the whipped cream for the fruit dessert, is a colorless, licorice-flavored beverage brewed from grape extracts and aromatic plants.

WHAT TO DRINK

A zesty, reasonably full-bodied red wine will stand up best to the lively flavors of this meal. A young California Zinfandel is an excellent choice.

SHOPPING LIST AND STAPLES

½ pound lean ground lamb
2 medium-size eggplants (about 1¾ pounds total weight)
Small head romaine lettuce
Medium-size green bell pepper
Medium-size red bell pepper
Hot cherry pepper (optional)
Small English cucumber or regular cucumber
2 medium-size onions
4 medium-size cloves garlic
Small bunch mint (optional)
Small cantaloupe
Small honeydew melon
Small lemon
2 eggs
2 cups milk
½ pint heavy cream
6 tablespoons unsalted butter
3 ounces Parmesan cheese, preferably imported
½ pint plain yogurt
1 cup good-quality olive oil, approximately
2 tablespoons tomato paste
½ cup plus 2 tablespoons all-purpose flour

41

Three 6-inch pita breads
2 teaspoons sesame seeds
2 tablespoons brown sugar
1 teaspoon dried oregano
1 teaspoon dried thyme
½ teaspoon dried basil
Salt
1 teaspoon kosher salt
Freshly ground black pepper
Freshly ground white pepper
2 tablespoons ouzo

UTENSILS

Food processor (optional)
Electric mixer
Large skillet
Small heavy-gauge nonaluminum saucepan
2-quart casserole or baking dish
15 x 10-inch baking sheet
2 large bowls
3 small bowls
Colander
Salad spinner (optional)
Strainer
Measuring cups and spoons
Chef's knife
Paring knife
2 wooden spoons
Slotted spoon
Metal spatula
Rubber spatula
Whisk
Grater
Vegetable peeler
Citrus juicer (optional)
Melon baller

START-TO-FINISH STEPS

The Day Before or the Morning of Serving
1. Peel garlic and mince 2 cloves for moussaka recipe, 1 clove for romaine recipe, and 1 clove for pita recipe. Set out butter to come to room temperature for pita recipe.
2. Follow melon recipe step 1, pita recipe step 1, and moussaka recipe step 1.
3. Follow romaine recipe step 1 and melon recipe step 2.
4. Follow pita recipe steps 2 through 5.
5. Follow moussaka recipe steps 2 through 8.
6. Follow romaine recipe steps 2 and 3 and melon recipe step 3.
7. Follow moussaka recipe steps 9 through 11.

Thirty Minutes Before Serving
1. Follow pita recipe step 6 and moussaka recipe steps 12 and 13.
2. Follow pita recipe step 7.
3. Follow romaine recipe step 4, pita recipe step 8, and

serve with moussaka.
4. Follow melon recipe steps 4 and 5 and serve for dessert.

RECIPES

Moussaka

2 medium-size eggplants (about 1¾ pounds total weight)
4 teaspoons salt, approximately
Medium-size green bell pepper
Medium-size red bell pepper
Hot cherry pepper (optional)
2 medium-size onions
3 ounces Parmesan cheese, preferably imported
¾ cup good-quality olive oil, approximately
2 medium-size cloves garlic, minced
½ pound lean ground lamb
2 tablespoons tomato paste
1 teaspoon dried oregano
½ teaspoon dried basil
Freshly ground black pepper
½ cup all-purpose flour

Béchamel Sauce:
2 tablespoons unsalted butter
2 tablespoons all-purpose flour
2 cups milk
2 eggs
½ teaspoon salt
Freshly ground white pepper

1. Wash eggplants and dry with paper towels. Trim but do not peel eggplants; cut crosswise into ½-inch-thick slices. Sprinkle slices with 4 teaspoons salt and allow to drain in colander 20 minutes.
2. Wash peppers and dry with paper towels. Halve, core, and seed bell peppers and cut into thin strips. If using cherry pepper, seed and chop finely.

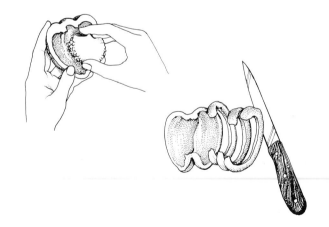

3. Peel and coarsely chop onions; you should have about 1¼ cups.
4. Using food processor or grater, grate enough Parmesan to measure ⅔ cup; set aside.
5. Heat 2 tablespoons olive oil in large skillet over medium heat until hot. Add peppers, onions, and garlic and cook 4

minutes, or until soft but not brown. Using slotted spoon, transfer vegetables to large bowl.

6. Add lamb to skillet and cook over medium-high heat, stirring often to break up any lumps, 5 minutes, or until meat is no longer pink.

7. Drain off excess fat. Return cooked vegetables to skillet with lamb and add tomato paste, oregano, basil, ⅓ cup Parmesan, and black pepper to taste. Stir to combine well. Transfer mixture to large bowl and wipe skillet with paper towels.

8. Spread ½ cup flour on sheet of waxed paper. Line large platter with paper towels. Heat 2 tablespoons olive oil in large skillet over medium-high heat until hot. Pat eggplant dry with paper towels and dredge slices lightly in flour. In batches, cook eggplant on both sides in skillet, adding more oil as necessary, 4 minutes, or until slightly browned. Transfer eggplant to paper-towel-lined platter.

9. For béchamel sauce, melt butter in small heavy-gauge nonaluminum saucepan over medium heat. Whisk in flour and cook, whisking continuously, 1 minute, or until bubbly. Gradually add milk and cook, stirring constantly, 3 to 5 minutes, or until mixture comes to a boil. Remove pan from heat.

10. Beat eggs in small bowl. Gradually add ½ cup hot milk mixture to eggs, stirring to combine well. Add egg mixture to mixture in saucepan and cook over low heat 1 minute. Add salt, and white pepper to taste.

11. Grease bottom and sides of 2-quart casserole or baking dish. Overlapping eggplant slices slightly, arrange half of eggplant in bottom of casserole. Cover with lamb mixture. Top with remaining eggplant. Pour béchamel sauce over eggplant and sprinkle with remaining Parmesan. Cover and refrigerate until 30 minutes before serving.

12. About 30 minutes before serving, preheat oven to 375 degrees.

13. Bake moussaka 30 minutes, or until sauce is bubbly and golden.

Romaine with Cucumber-Yogurt Dressing

Small English cucumber or regular cucumber
1 teaspoon kosher salt
½ cup plain yogurt
Medium-size clove garlic, minced
2 tablespoons good-quality olive oil
Freshly ground black pepper
Small head romaine lettuce

1. Peel cucumber. Using grater, coarsely shred enough cucumber to measure ½ cup. Reserve remainder for another use. Place shredded cucumber in strainer, sprinkle with salt, and set aside to drain at least 20 minutes.

2. After draining, combine cucumber, yogurt, garlic, olive oil, and pepper to taste in small bowl. Cover and refrigerate until just before serving.

3. Wash and dry romaine. Discard any bruised or discolored leaves and tear remaining lettuce into bite-size pieces. Wrap in paper towels, place in plastic bag, and refrigerate until just before serving.

4. To serve, place romaine in salad bowl, add dressing, and toss.

Romaine lettuce

Sesame Pita Crisps

Three 6-inch pita breads
Small lemon
4 tablespoons unsalted butter, at room temperature
2 teaspoons sesame seeds
Medium-size clove garlic, minced
1 teaspoon dried thyme

1. Preheat oven to 350 degrees.

2. Split each pita bread to form 2 rounds and quarter each round. Place pita on baking sheet and bake 7 to 8 minutes, or until dried. Remove from oven and let cool.

3. Meanwhile, halve lemon and squeeze enough juice to measure 1 tablespoon.

4. In small bowl, cream butter with sesame seeds, garlic, lemon juice, and thyme. Cover and refrigerate until 30 minutes before serving.

5. Place cooled pita in plastic bag until needed.

6. Thirty minutes before serving, set out butter mixture to come to room temperature.

7. Spread pita triangles with butter mixture and place on baking sheet.

8. Bake pita triangles in 350-degree oven 4 to 5 minutes, or until crisp and golden.

Melon with Ouzo Cream

Small cantaloupe
Small honeydew melon
1 cup heavy cream
2 tablespoons brown sugar
2 tablespoons ouzo
Small bunch mint for garnish (optional)

1. Place large bowl and beaters in freezer to chill.

2. Halve and seed melons. Using small melon baller, scoop out enough balls from each melon to measure a total of 3 cups. Place in serving bowl, cover, and refrigerate until 30 minutes before serving.

3. Remove bowl and beaters from freezer. Beat cream in chilled bowl with electric mixer 2 minutes, or until soft peaks form. Add brown sugar and ouzo and beat until stiff peaks form. Cover and refrigerate until ready to serve.

4. Just before serving, wash and dry 2 large mint sprigs, if using; reserve remaining mint for another use.

5. If cream has separated, whisk briefly to recombine. Top melon balls with cream and garnish with mint sprigs.

Roberta Rall

Home economist Roberta Rall asks herself three questions when she develops recipes: Does the recipe make efficient use of time and ingredients? Can the recipe teach the cook a new skill? And can the recipe, if complicated, be simplified so that even an inexperienced cook can prepare it? In the salmon and orzo salad of Menu 1, for example, she cooks the orzo in the same cooking liquid used for poaching the salmon, thus saving time and also enhancing the orzo's flavor. The herbed mustard sauce that dresses the salad doubles as a dip for the accompanying artichoke leaves.

In Menu 2, Roberta Rall marinates the seafood Provençal all day in the same parchment paper in which it is baked. "You can wrap the ingredients to be cooked in the parchment ahead of time," she says, "and the parchment will not get soggy." With the seafood she offers potato pancakes, which she reheats in the oven at the last minute to give them a crisp, golden crust.

Menu 3 features *raclette*, a cheese-and-vegetable dish traditionally prepared by melting a half wheel of cheese near an open fire, then scraping the softened cheese over vegetables. Here the cook melts the cheese in a saucepan with butter, flour, and seasonings, pours it over individual casseroles of vegetables and ham, then bakes the casseroles. With the *raclette* she serves a salad of sugar snap peas, mushrooms, and radishes, and for dessert, fruit wrapped and baked in filo dough.

Spinach and potato soup garnished with scallion greens and lemon rind complements a lavish salad of orzo and salmon surrounded by artichoke leaves.

45

Spinach and Potato Soup
Salmon and Orzo Sunburst Salad with Herbed Mustard Sauce

The showy salad makes full use of the artichoke: The hearts are chopped and mixed with the orzo and salmon, and the leaves form an attractive, edible sunburst around the pasta. Select firm, compact artichokes with fleshy leaves that close tightly around the central choke. To store artichokes, wrap them unwashed in a damp towel, then in a plastic bag, and refrigerate them for up to two days.

WHAT TO DRINK

A bright and acidic white wine is called for here. Choose a Sauvignon Blanc from California or Italy, or a Pouilly-Fumé or Sancerre from France.

SHOPPING LIST AND STAPLES

1½ pounds salmon fillets, 1 inch thick
Medium-size new potato (about 6 ounces)
1 pound spinach
Medium-size artichoke (about ¾ pound)
Medium-size tomato
Small bunch scallions
Small bunch parsley
Small bunch basil or dill, if available
Small bunch mint, plus additional bunch if not using basil or dill
2 small lemons
1 pint light cream or half-and-half
2 tablespoons unsalted butter
1 cup chicken stock, preferably homemade (see page 10), or canned
½ cup vegetable oil
¼ cup white wine vinegar or balsamic vinegar
½ cup coarse-grain Dijon mustard
8-ounce package orzo
3 tablespoons brown sugar, approximately
1 bay leaf
⅛ teaspoon nutmeg
½ teaspoon whole black peppercorns
Salt and freshly ground white pepper
½ cup dry white wine

UTENSILS

Food processor or blender
Large nonaluminum skillet
Heavy-gauge stockpot with cover
Large saucepan with cover
2 large bowls, 1 nonaluminum
Small bowl
Salad spinner (optional)
Colander
Measuring cups and spoons
Chef's knife
Paring knife
2 wooden spoons
Slotted spoon
Slotted spatula
Rubber spatula
Citrus juicer (optional)
Whisk

START-TO-FINISH STEPS

The Morning of Serving
1. Follow soup recipe steps 1 through 4.
2. While potato is cooking, follow salad recipe steps 1 through 5.
3. While salmon and artichoke are cooking, follow soup recipe steps 5 and 6.
4. Follow salad recipe steps 6 through 8.
5. While orzo is cooking, follow sauce recipe steps 1 and 2.
6. Follow salad recipe steps 9 and 10.

Fifteen Minutes Before Serving
1. Follow salad recipe steps 11 through 14, soup recipe steps 7 and 8, and serve.

RECIPES

Spinach and Potato Soup

Medium-size new potato (about 6 ounces)
4 medium-size scallions
Small lemon
1 pound spinach
Small bunch mint
2 tablespoons unsalted butter
1 cup chicken stock
⅛ teaspoon nutmeg
¼ teaspoon freshly ground white pepper
1¼ cups light cream or half-and-half

1. Scrub and rinse potato; do not peel. Wash scallions and

lemon and dry with paper towels. Cut potato into ½-inch dice. Reserve one scallion for garnish. Cut enough remaining scallions into 2-inch pieces to measure ¾ cup. Using sharp paring knife, remove two 1-inch-wide strips of lemon rind; wrap and reserve for garnish. Halve lemon and squeeze enough juice to measure 2 teaspoons.

2. Remove and discard tough stems from spinach. Wash spinach in several changes of cold water and dry in salad spinner or with paper towels. Wash and dry mint; set aside ¼ cup loosely packed mint leaves.

Fresh mint

3. Melt butter in heavy-gauge stockpot over medium heat. Add scallion pieces and cook 2 minutes.

4. Add potato, stock, and 1 cup hot water and bring to a boil. Cover pot and cook over medium heat 12 minutes, or until potato is just tender.

5. Add spinach and cook, covered, 3 minutes, or just until wilted. Transfer mixture to food processor or blender and add 3 tablespoons mint leaves, lemon juice, nutmeg, and pepper. Process briefly until smooth.

6. Pour mixture into large nonaluminum bowl and stir in cream or half-and-half. Cut remaining mint into thin strips and stir into soup. Cover bowl and refrigerate until just before serving.

7. Just before serving, cut green part of reserved scallion and lemon rind into thin strips.

8. Stir soup and divide among 4 soup bowls. Garnish with strips of scallion green and lemon rind.

Salmon and Orzo Sunburst Salad

Small lemon
Medium-size artichoke (about ¾ pound)
1½ pounds salmon fillets, 1 inch thick
½ cup dry white wine
½ teaspoon whole black peppercorns
1 bay leaf
½ teaspoon salt
1½ cups orzo
Herbed Mustard Sauce (see following recipe)
Medium-size tomato

1. Bring 6 cups water to a boil in large saucepan over high heat.

2. Meanwhile, cut waxed-paper disk to fit large non-aluminum skillet. Wash lemon and artichoke and dry with paper towels. Halve lemon and cut 1 half into slices. Set

aside other half. Trim stem and tough outer leaves from artichoke.

3. Wipe salmon with damp paper towels. Combine 2 cups water, wine, lemon slices, peppercorns, bay leaf, and salt in large nonaluminum skillet. Bring mixture to a boil over high heat.

4. Add salmon and cover with waxed paper. Return liquid to a boil, reduce heat to medium, and poach salmon 12 to 15 minutes, or just until fish flakes.

5. Meanwhile, halve artichoke and rub cut surfaces with reserved lemon half. Add artichoke halves and lemon half to boiling water in large saucepan. Cover pan and cook artichoke over medium heat 10 minutes, or until tender when pierced near stem end with fork.

6. Drain artichoke halves, wrap tightly in plastic, and refrigerate until 15 minutes before serving.

7. Using slotted spatula, transfer salmon to plate to cool. Using slotted spoon, remove and discard lemon slices, peppercorns, and bay leaf from cooking liquid.

8. Add orzo to cooking liquid and bring to a boil over medium-high heat. Cook orzo, stirring occasionally, 10 to 12 minutes, or until tender. Add additional hot water if necessary.

9. Rinse orzo in colander under cold running water; drain. Turn orzo into large bowl, cover with plastic wrap, and refrigerate until 15 minutes before serving.

10. Skin salmon and break into bite-size chunks, discarding any bones. Cover with plastic wrap and refrigerate until 15 minutes before serving.

11. To serve, remove orzo from refrigerator. Fold in salmon and ⅔ cup herbed mustard sauce.

12. Remove leaves from artichoke halves and arrange around outside edge of serving platter. Remove and discard fuzzy choke from each half. Chop artichoke heart and add to salmon and orzo mixture. Mix gently with fork.

13. Wash and dry tomato. If making tomato rose for garnish, use sharp paring knife to peel tomato skin in one continuous ¼- to ½-inch-wide strip. Roll strip into rose shape. (See also page TK.) If not making rose, do not peel tomato. Cut tomato into 1-inch pieces and add to salad.

14. Spoon salad onto center of platter and garnish with tomato rose, if desired. Serve remaining herbed mustard sauce separately as dipping sauce for artichoke leaves.

Herbed Mustard Sauce

Small bunch parsley
Small bunch basil, dill, or mint
½ cup coarse-grain Dijon mustard
½ cup vegetable oil
¼ cup white wine vinegar or balsamic vinegar
2 to 3 tablespoons brown sugar

1. Wash and dry herbs. Mince enough parsley to measure ¼ cup. Mince enough basil, dill, or mint to measure ¼ cup. Reserve remaining herbs for another use.

2. Combine herbs, mustard, oil, vinegar, and sugar in small bowl and whisk until smooth. Cover and refrigerate until 15 minutes before serving.

Seafood Provençal in Parchment
Lacy Potato Pancakes
Honeydew-Avocado Salad

Let your guests open their own individual packets of seafood Provençal at the table. Serve the seafood with potato pancakes and a decorative salad of endive, melon balls, avocado slices, and hazelnuts.

For an impressive company dinner that looks complicated but is not, present the seafood Provençal in the individual parchment packets in which it cooks. Kitchen parchment, sold at specialty food shops and kitchen supply stores, preserves the natural moisture and nutrient content of foods and also cuts down on clean-up time. As the packets heat up, some steam escapes through the porous paper, thereby preventing the food from becoming soggy. Serve the packets unopened so the food stays hot; then, snip them open at the table to release a mouth-watering burst of aroma.

WHAT TO DRINK

Serve this seafood dinner with a delicate and fruity white Riesling from the Pacific Northwest or Alsace. Or, for a slightly sweeter taste, choose a Riesling from one of Germany's Rhine districts.

SHOPPING LIST AND STAPLES

4 fillets of sole (about 1½ pounds total weight)
12 large shrimp
¼ pound bay scallops
1 pound Russet potatoes
2 medium-size tomatoes (about 1 pound total weight)
Small zucchini
¼ pound small fresh mushrooms
Small head Boston lettuce
Medium-size head Belgian endive
Small bunch scallions
Small onion
Large shallot
Medium-size clove garlic
Small bunch basil
Small bunch parsley
Small honeydew melon
Small avocado
Large lemon
1 lime
2 eggs
5 tablespoons unsalted butter, approximately
½ cup vegetable oil, approximately
2 tablespoons hazelnut or walnut oil
1 teaspoon Dijon mustard
¼ cup all-purpose flour
¼ cup hazelnuts or walnuts

¼ teaspoon dried thyme
1 bay leaf
Salt and freshly ground black and white pepper

UTENSILS

Food processor (optional)
Large skillet
Large shallow skillet or griddle
Large saucepan
3 baking sheets
2 large bowls
Medium-size nonaluminum bowl
Small nonaluminum bowl
Salad spinner (optional)
Colander
Measuring cups and spoons
Chef's knife
Paring knife
2 wooden spoons
Slotted spoon
Slotted spatula
Grater
Vegetable peeler
Whisk
Melon baller
Parchment paper

START-TO-FINISH STEPS

The Morning of Serving

1. Wash lemon and dry with paper towel. Grate enough lemon rind to measure 1 teaspoon for seafood recipe. Halve lemon and squeeze enough juice to measure 2 tablespoons for pancakes recipe and 4 teaspoons for seafood recipe. Halve lime and squeeze enough juice to measure 2½ tablespoons for salad recipe.
2. Follow seafood recipe steps 1 through 9.

Up to Six Hours Before Serving

1. Follow pancakes recipe steps 1 through 7.

Thirty Minutes Before Serving

1. Follow seafood recipe step 10 and salad recipe step 1.
2. Follow seafood recipe step 11.
3. While seafood is baking, follow salad recipe steps 2 through 7.
4. Follow pancakes recipe step 8 and salad recipe steps 8 and 9.
5. Follow seafood recipe step 12, pancakes recipe step 9, and serve with salad.

RECIPES

Seafood Provençal in Parchment

Small onion
Medium-size clove garlic

2 medium-size tomatoes (about 1 pound total weight)
Small zucchini
Small bunch basil
Small bunch parsley
¼ pound small fresh mushrooms
2 tablespoons unsalted butter
Salt
Freshly ground white pepper
¼ teaspoon dried thyme
1 bay leaf
1 teaspoon grated lemon rind
12 large shrimp
4 fillets of sole (about 1½ pounds total weight)
4 teaspoons lemon juice
¼ pound bay scallops

1. Bring 6 cups water to a boil in large saucepan over high heat.
2. Meanwhile, cut 4 pieces of parchment paper into heart shapes about 12 inches deep and 12 inches wide at top. Set aside.
3. Peel and chop onion. Peel and mince garlic. Wash tomatoes, zucchini, and fresh herbs, and dry with paper towels. Cut zucchini crosswise into thin slices. Mince enough basil and parsley to measure ¼ cup each; set aside.
4. Wipe mushrooms clean with damp paper towel and slice thinly.
5. Fill large bowl with ice water. Drop tomatoes into boiling water and blanch 30 seconds. With slotted spoon, transfer tomatoes briefly to bowl of ice water. Drain tomatoes and peel; halve crosswise and squeeze out seeds. Cut tomatoes into chunks.
6. Melt butter in large skillet over medium heat. Add onion and garlic and cook 2 minutes, or until onion is tender. Stir in tomatoes, zucchini, basil, parsley, mushrooms, ¼ teaspoon salt, ⅛ teaspoon white pepper, thyme, bay leaf, and lemon rind. Bring to a boil and simmer gently, stirring occasionally, 10 minutes, or until sauce is thickened.
7. Meanwhile, pinch legs off shrimp, several at a time, then bend back and snap off sharp, beaklike pieces of shell just above tail. Leaving tail intact, remove shell and discard. Using sharp paring knife, make shallow incision along back of each shrimp, exposing digestive vein. Extract vein and discard.

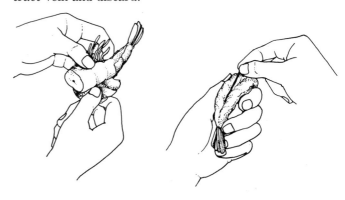

8. Wipe sole fillets with damp paper towels. Place 1 fillet to one side of center on each parchment-paper heart, tucking under thin ends of fillets. Sprinkle each fillet with 1 teaspoon lemon juice and season with salt and pepper. Place 3 shrimp and one fourth of scallops on and around each fillet. Remove and discard bay leaf from sauce and top seafood with equal portions of sauce.

9. Fold parchment paper over filling, bringing halves of heart together. Seal packages by starting at "V" in heart and rolling and crimping edges together tightly. Twist tip of heart to seal. Place packets on baking sheet and refrigerate until 30 minutes before serving.

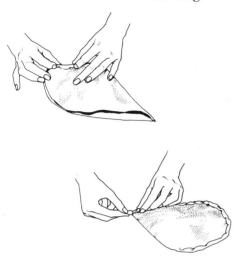

10. Thirty minutes before serving, preheat oven to 425 degrees.

11. Bake packets 25 minutes.

12. To serve, place a packet on each of 4 dinner plates.

Lacy Potato Pancakes

3 medium-size scallions
1 pound Russet potatoes
2 tablespoons lemon juice
¼ cup all-purpose flour
2 eggs
½ teaspoon salt
⅛ teaspoon freshly ground black pepper
3 tablespoons unsalted butter, approximately
3 tablespoons vegetable oil, approximately

1. Wash scallions and dry with paper towel. Thinly slice enough scallions to measure ¼ cup; set aside.

2. Peel potatoes. In food processor, or with grater, shred enough potatoes to measure about 2½ cups. Place in medium-size nonaluminum bowl. Add lemon juice and enough water to cover; stir well.

3. Turn potatoes into colander and drain well. Turn out potatoes onto paper towels and thoroughly pat dry.

4. Combine scallions, flour, eggs, salt, and pepper in large bowl. Stir in potatoes.

5. In large shallow skillet or on griddle, heat 1 tablespoon butter and 1 tablespoon oil over medium heat until hot. Add potato mixture by scant quarter-cupsful, spreading

mixture to make thin pancakes (small holes will form). Do not crowd. Cook pancakes 3 to 4 minutes, turning once.

6. Using slotted spatula, transfer pancakes to baking sheet in single layer. Repeat procedure with remaining potato mixture, stirring well before measuring out each portion. Add additional butter and oil as needed.

7. Allow pancakes to cool, cover with plastic wrap, and let stand at room temperature until 10 minutes before serving. Do not let potatoes sit out for more than 6 hours.

8. To serve, heat pancakes in 425-degree oven 8 to 10 minutes, or until golden brown and crisp.

9. Divide pancakes among 4 dinner plates.

Honeydew-Avocado Salad

Large shallot
¼ cup hazelnuts or walnuts
Small avocado
¼ cup vegetable oil
2 tablespoons hazelnut or walnut oil
2½ tablespoons lime juice
1 teaspoon Dijon mustard
⅛ teaspoon salt
⅛ teaspoon freshly ground black pepper
Small head Boston lettuce
Medium-size head Belgian endive
Small honeydew melon

1. Peel and mince shallot; set aside.

2. If using hazelnuts, place on baking sheet and toast in 425-degree oven, stirring occasionally, 5 to 7 minutes, or until skins split.

3. Meanwhile, halve and pit avocado. Peel halves and cut into ½-inch-wide slices.

4. Combine shallot, oils, lime juice, mustard, salt, and pepper in small nonaluminum bowl and whisk to blend. Add avocado slices and turn to coat with dressing. Set aside.

5. Remove hazelnuts from oven and set aside to cool.

6. Wash lettuce; discard any bruised or discolored leaves. Trim endive and separate leaves. Dry lettuce and endive in salad spinner or with paper towels; set aside.

7. Halve and seed honeydew. Using melon baller, cut enough fruit into balls to measure about 3 cups. Reserve remaining melon for another use.

8. Place hazelnuts in kitchen towel and rub between hands to remove skins. Coarsely chop hazelnuts or walnuts.

9. Line 4 salad plates with lettuce. Arrange endive, avocado, and melon balls decoratively on lettuce. Stir dressing and drizzle over salads. Sprinkle with nuts and serve.

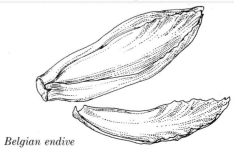

Belgian endive

Raclette Casseroles
Marinated Vegetable Salad
Fruit in Filo Bundles

Piping hot raclette *casseroles, a vegetable salad with sugar snap peas, and fruit-filled filo for dessert make an elegant supper.*

*R*aclette (from the French verb *racler*, "to scrape") is best if you use authentic Swiss *raclette* cheese, which has a firm texture and a mild nutty taste. If it is unavailable, substitute another mild, easy-melting cheese such as Swiss, Jarlsberg, or Gruyère.

The fruit-filled filo bundles are perfect for make-ahead meals because they can be prepared up to 24 hours in advance and held in the refrigerator until you are ready to bake them. (See page 39 for information on thawing and using filo dough.) Vary the fruit filling according to the season; for example, you can use fresh peaches instead of the pears and apples.

WHAT TO DRINK

A full-bodied white California Chardonnay or a good French Chablis would be an excellent selection here.

SHOPPING LIST AND STAPLES

¾ pound Black Forest ham, in one piece
1½ pounds small new red potatoes
Small bunch broccoli (about 1 pound)
½ pound sugar snap peas or green beans
¼ pound fresh mushrooms

Small bunch radishes
Small head romaine lettuce
Small red onion
Large lemon
2 large pears (about 1 pound total weight)
Large Granny Smith apple
2 eggs
1¼ cups milk or half-and-half
1 stick plus 6 tablespoons unsalted butter
½ pound raclette cheese
½-pound package frozen filo dough
½ cup vegetable oil
1 teaspoon Dijon mustard
¼ cup all-purpose flour
½ cup plus 2 teaspoons sugar
9-ounce box dark raisins
¾ teaspoon cinnamon
⅛ teaspoon nutmeg, approximately
Salt and freshly ground black pepper

UTENSILS

Food processor or blender
Large saucepan
Medium-size saucepan with cover
Two small saucepans
Collapsible vegetable steamer
15 x 10-inch baking sheet
4 individual casseroles
Large nonaluminum bowl
Medium-size bowl
2 small bowls
Colander
Measuring cups and spoons
Chef's knife
Paring knife
Wooden spoon
Wide metal spatula
Grater
Vegetable peeler
Pastry brush

START-TO-FINISH STEPS

The Morning of Serving

1. Wash lemon. Grate enough rind to measure 1 teaspoon each for salad and filo bundles recipes. Halve lemon; squeeze enough juice to measure 1 tablespoon for salad recipe.
2. Follow filo bundles recipe steps 1 through 7.
3. Follow salad recipe steps 1 through 9.
4. Follow raclette recipe steps 1 through 7.

Thirty Minutes Before Serving

1. Follow raclette recipe steps 8 through 12.
2. Follow salad recipe steps 10 and 11.
3. Follow raclette recipe step 13, filo bundles recipe step 8, and serve raclette casseroles with salad.
4. Follow filo bundles recipe step 9 and serve for dessert.

52

RECIPES

Raclette Casseroles

1½ pounds small new red potatoes
¾ pound Black Forest ham, in one piece
Salt
Small bunch broccoli (about 1 pound)
½ pound raclette cheese
2 tablespoons unsalted butter
2 tablespoons all-purpose flour
1¼ cups milk or half-and-half
⅛ teaspoon freshly ground black pepper
Pinch of nutmeg

1. Bring 2 quarts water to a boil in large saucepan over high heat.
2. Meanwhile, scrub and dry potatoes and cut into ½-inch-thick slices. You should have about 5 cups. Cut ham into 1-inch cubes; set aside.
3. Add ½ teaspoon salt and potatoes to boiling water. Boil, stirring occasionally, 8 minutes.
4. Meanwhile, wash and dry broccoli. Cut broccoli tops into florets. Reserve stems for another use.
5. When potatoes have cooked 8 minutes, add broccoli, reduce heat to medium-low, and simmer 5 minutes, or until potatoes and broccoli are tender.
6. Turn vegetables into colander to drain and cool.
7. When cooled, place potatoes, broccoli, and ham in plastic bag. Close bag tightly and refrigerate until 30 minutes before serving.
8. Thirty minutes before serving, preheat oven to 400 degrees. Grease 4 individual heatproof casseroles.
9. Cut enough cheese into 1-inch cubes to measure 2 cups. Cut remaining cheese into thin strips and set aside.
10. Melt butter over medium heat in small saucepan. Stir in flour, then gradually add milk or half-and-half. Stirring constantly, cook 1 minute, or until smooth. Add ¼ teaspoon salt, pepper, and nutmeg and continue to cook over medium heat, stirring occasionally, 3 to 4 minutes, or until mixture comes just to a boil. Remove from heat and stir in cheese cubes.
11. Divide half of potatoes, broccoli, and ham among individual casseroles. Spoon ¼ cup sauce into each casserole and top with remaining vegetables and ham. Spoon remaining sauce over top.
12. Bake raclettes 15 minutes.
13. Top raclettes with reserved cheese strips and bake another 5 minutes, or until bubbling.

Marinated Vegetable Salad

½ pound sugar snap peas or green beans
6 radishes
Small red onion
2 eggs
¼ pound fresh mushrooms
1 tablespoon lemon juice
1 teaspoon grated lemon rind

1 teaspoon Dijon mustard
½ teaspoon salt
⅛ teaspoon freshly ground black pepper
½ cup vegetable oil
Small head romaine lettuce

1. Wash, dry, and trim peas or beans and radishes. If using beans, cut into 3-inch lengths. Thinly slice radishes. Peel and thinly slice onion. Place radishes and onion in large nonaluminum bowl.
2. Separate eggs, placing yolks in small bowl and reserving whites for another use.
3. Bring 1 inch water to a boil in medium-size saucepan fitted with vegetable steamer.
4. Meanwhile, wipe mushrooms clean with damp paper towel and cut into ¼-inch-thick slices. Add to bowl with radishes and onion.
5. Place peas or beans in steamer, cover pan, and steam 3 minutes.
6. Meanwhile, in food processor or blender, combine egg yolks, lemon juice, lemon rind, mustard, salt, and pepper. Process 10 seconds, or until combined. With machine running, add oil in a slow, steady stream.
7. Transfer peas or beans to colander, refresh under cold running water, and allow to drain.
8. Add peas or beans to large bowl.
9. Drizzle dressing over vegetables, toss to combine, cover, and refrigerate until just before serving.
10. To serve, wash lettuce and dry with paper towels. Discard any bruised or discolored leaves. Line salad bowl with lettuce leaves.
11. Gently toss marinated vegetables and add to salad bowl.

Fruit in Filo Bundles

¾ cup unsalted butter
2 large pears (about 1 pound total weight)
Large Granny Smith apple
½ cup plus 2 teaspoons sugar
¼ cup dark raisins
2 tablespoons all-purpose flour
1 teaspoon grated lemon rind
¾ teaspoon cinnamon
⅛ teaspoon nutmeg
16 sheets filo, thawed

1. Lightly grease baking sheet. Melt butter in small saucepan over medium-low heat.
2. Peel pears and apple. Core fruit and cut into wedges, then cut crosswise into ⅛-inch-thick slices.
3. Combine ½ cup sugar, raisins, flour, lemon rind, ½ teaspoon cinnamon, and nutmeg in medium-size bowl.
4. Add fruit and toss to coat well.
5. Place filo sheets on a damp towel covered with plastic wrap and cover top sheet with plastic wrap and a second damp towel. To make one bundle, lay 1 sheet flat on work surface and brush lightly with melted butter. Top with second sheet and brush lightly with butter. Repeat proce-

dure with third sheet. Fold fourth sheet in half and center on stack. Brush lightly with butter and spoon one fourth of fruit filling onto center of folded sheet.
6. Fold over long sides of filo to cover fruit. Fold over short sides, twisting edges in center to close bundle. Brush with butter and transfer to prepared baking sheet. Make 3 more bundles in same manner.
7. Combine remaining 2 teaspoons sugar and ¼ teaspoon cinnamon in small bowl. Sprinkle over bundles, cover pan, and refrigerate until 30 minutes before serving.
8. To bake, place bundles in 400-degree oven for 25 minutes, or until golden brown.
9. Using wide metal spatula, transfer filo bundles to napkin-lined platter, and serve hot.

ADDED TOUCH

These ultra-crisp breadsticks made with pumpernickel rye flour can be topped with coarse salt or caraway seeds before baking. Or try fennel or anise seeds.

Pumpernickel Breadsticks

1¼ cups all-purpose flour, approximately
1 cup pumpernickel rye flour, or regular rye flour
1 packet (¼ ounce) fast-acting yeast
1 tablespoon brown sugar
1 tablespoon unsweetened cocoa powder
1 teaspoon salt
¼ cup vegetable oil
1 tablespoon molasses
¼ cup cornmeal
1 egg white
Kosher salt or caraway seeds

1. In food processor fitted with dough blade, combine flours, yeast, sugar, cocoa, and salt. Process 10 seconds, or until combined. With machine running, gradually add ¼ cup hot tap water. Or, combine ingredients in large bowl and stir with wooden spoon.
2. Combine ½ cup cold water, oil, and molasses in small bowl. With processor running, gradually add mixture and process until dough forms a ball. Or, add molasses mixture to large bowl and stir with wooden spoon. (Dough will be quite sticky. If it is too sticky to handle, add 1 tablespoon flour. If it is too dry, add 1 teaspoon water.)
3. Process or stir 1 minute more to knead dough. Let dough rest 20 minutes. Meanwhile, sprinkle two 17 x 11-inch baking sheets with cornmeal.
4. Transfer dough to lightly floured surface. Halve dough and cut each half into 16 pieces. Roll each piece into a 7-inch stick. Arrange sticks 1 inch apart on baking sheets. Cover sheets with kitchen towels and let rise in warm place 30 minutes.
5. Preheat oven to 350 degrees.
6. Lightly beat egg white with 1 teaspoon water in small bowl. Brush breadsticks with egg white and sprinkle with kosher salt or caraway seeds. Bake 30 minutes, or until crisp. Transfer to rack to cool.

Gloria Zimmerman

MENU 1 (Left)
Thai Seafood Soup
Ginger Chicken
White Rice

MENU 2
Vietnamese Salad
Poached Chicken with Rice and Ginger Sauce

MENU 3
Sour Beef Salad
Sweet Pork
Broccoli with Oyster Sauce

When Gloria Zimmerman was learning to cook Thai and Vietnamese dishes, she needed a teacher to explain the ingredients to her and a translator to help her order them in the ethnic markets, where no one spoke English. Today, to her delight, many more sources—including mail order (see page 103)—offer the exotic ingredients required by these two cuisines. Here she presents two Thai menus and one from Vietnam, all featuring intriguing combinations of colors and flavors—and all suited for make-ahead meals. Although Gloria Zimmerman suggests alternatives for those ingredients that may be hard to get, she strongly recommends using ethnic products to achieve authentic results.

In Menu 1, she prepares a Thai seafood soup call *po taek*. This rich combination of shrimp, fish, mussels, and squid is flavored with lemon grass and other Thai seasonings and is followed by a main course of chicken cooked with ginger.

A Vietnamese meal, Menu 2 begins with a salad of pork, whole shrimp, and egg strips served over bean sprouts and marinated onions. Although the salad might seem like a meal in itself, in Vietnam it is typically followed by a meat course. Here the cook offers poached chicken bathed in a spicy ginger-garlic sauce.

In Menu 3, the steak for the Thai sour beef salad is broiled early on the day of serving, then, just before dinnertime, sliced and flavored with fish sauce, lime juice, and hot red or green chili peppers if desired. Sweetened pork slices and broccoli with oyster sauce provide interesting flavor contrasts to the beef. You can also serve rice with this meal.

The Thai seafood soup is a beautiful mix of tastes and textures. As additional seasonings, offer lime juice, fish sauce, and red pepper flakes on the side. Present the ginger chicken and rice after the soup.

55

Thai Seafood Soup
Ginger Chicken
White Rice

The seafood soup contains a number of ingredients used frequently in Thai cooking, among them lemon grass, dried *galangal* (also known as *kha*), and dried keffir lime leaves (*makrut*). Lemon grass is a tall woody grass resembling a large scallion, with an intriguing sour taste. Sometimes available fresh, but more often dried, lemon grass is sold in Asian groceries. If you buy fresh, use only the portion of the stalk up to the point where the gray-green leaves begin to branch off. If you use dried lemon grass, wrap it in cheesecloth for cooking and discard it before serving. An acceptable substitute is the rind from half a lemon.

Galangal (or *galingale*) is a rhizome, like ginger, but with a more delicate taste. Dried *galangal* is inexpensive and can be bought at Thai groceries. If it is unavailable, substitute a half-inch piece of ginger. The lime leaves come from the keffir lime tree. Most Oriental markets sell the leaves dried; Thai groceries often stock them frozen. As an alternative, you can use fresh lemon or lime leaves or the rind from half a lime.

The chicken dish gains an interesting texture with the addition of tree ear (also known as cloud ear) mushrooms. Sold dried, these fairly bland mushrooms expand to five or six times their original size when soaked. If they are unavailable, omit them from the recipe.

WHAT TO DRINK

Dark, full-bodied beer, served ice cold, is the best beverage for these spicy dishes. Try a Japanese or Mexican brand.

SHOPPING LIST AND STAPLES

1 pound boneless, skinless chicken breasts
1 pound mussels, or ½ pound crabmeat
½ pound medium-size shrimp
½ pound squid, cleaned
¾ pound haddock, sole, or flounder fillets, preferably with skin
Medium-size clove garlic
2-inch piece fresh ginger, or 2½-inch piece if not using galangal
2 stalks fresh or dried lemon grass, if available
Medium-size lemon (if not using lemon grass)
3 large limes

15-ounce can straw mushrooms
2 tablespoons vegetable oil
6-ounce bottle Thai fish sauce (nam pla), if available
2 tablespoons dark soy sauce, plus ¾ cup if not using fish sauce
1½ cups long-grain white rice
2 teaspoons sugar
2 ounces dried tree ear mushrooms, if available
6 slices dried galangal, if available
5 dried keffir lime leaves, if available
Red pepper flakes (optional)
Salt

UTENSILS

Wok or large heavy-gauge skillet
5-quart saucepan with cover
Medium-size saucepan with cover
Large bowl
Medium-size bowl
Small bowl
Colander
Strainer
Measuring cups and spoons
Chef's knife
Paring knife
Cooking spoon
Wooden spoon
Ladle
Cheesecloth (optional)
Kitchen string (optional)
Stiff-bristled brush

START-TO-FINISH STEPS

The Day Before or the Morning of Serving
1. Follow chicken recipe step 1 and soup recipe steps 1 through 3.
2. Follow chicken recipe steps 2 through 5.
3. Follow soup recipe steps 4 through 7.

Thirty Minutes Before Serving
1. Follow soup recipe step 8 and rice recipe steps 1 and 2.
2. While rice is cooking, follow soup recipe steps 9 through 12 and serve as first course.
3. Follow chicken recipe step 6, rice recipe step 3, and serve.

Thai Seafood Soup

2 stalks fresh or dried lemon grass, cut into 2-inch
    sections, or rind of ½ lemon
15-ounce can straw mushrooms
6 slices dried galangal, or ½-inch piece fresh ginger,
    peeled and thinly sliced
5 dried keffir lime leaves, or rind of ½ lime
1 pound mussels, or ½ pound crabmeat
½ pound medium-size shrimp
½ pound squid, cleaned
¾ pound haddock, sole, or flounder fillets, preferably
    with skin
3 large limes
¾ cup Thai fish sauce (nam pla) or soy sauce
Red pepper flakes (optional)

1. Bring 6 cups water to a boil in 5-quart saucepan over high heat.
2. Meanwhile, wrap dried lemon grass, if using, in piece of cheesecloth and tie securely with kitchen string. Drain mushrooms in colander.
3. Add lemon grass or lemon rind, straw mushrooms, galangal or sliced ginger, and lime leaves or lime rind to boiling water. Boil 5 minutes, or until stock becomes aromatic. Remove pan from heat and, when stock has cooled, cover and refrigerate until 30 minutes before serving.
4. Scrub mussels, if using, and remove hairlike beards. Rinse mussels and place in large bowl. Cover, and refrigerate until 30 minutes before serving.
5. Peel and devein shrimp (see page 49), leaving tails intact. Place shrimp in medium-size bowl, cover, and refrigerate until 30 minutes before serving.
6. Separate squid tentacles from body sac. Cut body sac open lengthwise and lay flat, fleshier side up. Without cutting through flesh completely, score diagonally in both directions. If squid is large, halve lengthwise. Wrap in plastic and refrigerate until 30 minutes before serving.
7. Wipe fish fillets with damp paper towels. Cut fillets into 2-inch-long by 1-inch-wide pieces. Wrap in plastic and refrigerate until 30 minutes before serving.
8. Thirty minutes before serving, bring stock to a simmer over medium heat.
9. Add squid and return soup to a simmer. Add mussels or crabmeat and return soup to a simmer. Add pieces of fish and return soup to a simmer.

10. Skim froth from soup. Cover pan and simmer 2 minutes, or until seafood is completely cooked. Discard any unopened mussels. Meanwhile, halve and juice limes.
11. Add 3 tablespoons fish sauce or soy sauce and ¼ cup lime juice to soup and stir. Place remaining fish sauce, remaining lime juice, and red pepper flakes if using in small bowls to serve as condiments.
12. Ladle soup into large serving bowl or tureen or into 4 individual soup bowls and serve with condiments.

Ginger Chicken

2 tablespoons dried tree ear mushrooms (optional)
1 pound boneless, skinless chicken breasts
Medium-size clove garlic
2-inch piece fresh ginger
2 tablespoons vegetable oil
2 teaspoons sugar
2 tablespoons dark soy sauce

1. If using mushrooms, place in small bowl, add hot water to cover, and let soak 20 minutes.
2. Cut chicken into 1-inch pieces. Peel and mince garlic. Peel ginger and cut lengthwise into thin strips.
3. Drain mushrooms in strainer; discard liquid. Rinse mushrooms well and pat dry with paper towels.
4. Heat oil in wok or large heavy-gauge skillet over medium heat until hot. Add garlic and stir fry 30 seconds, or until golden brown. Add chicken and stir fry 3 minutes, or until flesh is opaque.
5. Add ginger and stir fry 1 minute. Add mushrooms, if using, and stir well. Stir in sugar and soy sauce and remove wok or skillet from heat. When cooled, cover pan with foil and refrigerate until just before serving.
6. To serve, reheat chicken over medium heat, stirring often, 3 to 4 minutes, or until hot. Transfer to platter.

White Rice

¼ teaspoon salt
1½ cups long-grain white rice

1. Bring 3 cups water and salt to a boil in medium-size saucepan over high heat.
2. Stir in rice, cover pan, and reduce heat to medium-low. Simmer gently 18 to 20 minutes, or until rice is tender and water is completely absorbed.
3. Fluff rice with fork and transfer to serving dish.

Vietnamese Salad
Poached Chicken with Rice and Ginger Sauce

A Vietnamese tiered salad of bean sprouts, onion, pork, shrimp, and strips of egg piques the appetite for chicken in a spicy sauce.

The dressing for the salad is a classic Vietnamese sauce called *nuoc cham*. It is made with *nuoc nam*, an aromatic fish-based condiment that is as basic to Vietnamese cooking as salt is to Western cuisines. *Nuoc nam* and the similar Thai fish sauce *nam pla* (an acceptable substitute) are sold bottled in Oriental groceries. The word *nhi* on the Vietnamese product indicates that it is of highest quality.

WHAT TO DRINK

Beer or ale suits this menu well. If you prefer wine, a simple dry white, well chilled, would be your best bet. Try a Soave or a Spanish white Rioja.

SHOPPING LIST AND STAPLES

6 ounces boneless pork loin roast
3-pound chicken, quartered
¼ pound medium-size shrimp
1 pound bean sprouts
Small cucumber
Small carrot
Medium-size onion

4 medium-size cloves garlic
2-inch piece fresh ginger
Small bunch coriander
Small bunch mint
Large lime
1 egg
1 tablespoon plus ½ teaspoon vegetable oil
½ cup plus 3 tablespoons distilled white vinegar
6-ounce bottle Vietnamese fish sauce (nuoc nam) or
 ¼ cup dark soy sauce
1½ cups long-grain white rice
8-ounce jar dry-roasted peanuts (optional)
½ cup sugar, approximately
¾ teaspoon red pepper flakes
Salt
Freshly ground black pepper

UTENSILS

2 large stockpots, 1 with cover
8-inch skillet
3-quart saucepan with cover
2 small saucepans, 1 with cover, 1 nonaluminum
2 large bowls
3 small bowls, 2 nonaluminum
Colander
Strainer
Measuring cups and spoons
Chef's knife
Paring knife
Metal spatula
Wooden spoon
Grater
Citrus juicer (optional)
Mortar and pestle
Metal tongs

START-TO-FINISH STEPS

The Day Before or the Morning of Serving
1. Halve lime and squeeze enough juice to measure 2 tablespoons for ginger sauce recipe and 1 tablespoon for salad recipe.
2. Follow chicken recipe step 1 and salad recipe steps 1 through 3.
3. Follow chicken recipe step 2.
4. While chicken is poaching, follow salad recipe steps 4 through 10 and ginger sauce recipe steps 1 and 2.
5. Follow chicken recipe steps 3 and 4 and salad recipe steps 11 through 13.
6. Follow chicken recipe step 5 and salad recipe step 14.

Thirty Minutes Before Serving
1. Follow salad recipe step 15 and chicken recipe steps 6 through 11.
2. While rice and chicken are cooking, follow salad recipe steps 16 through 18 and serve as first course.
3. Follow chicken recipe step 12 and serve.

RECIPES

Vietnamese Salad

6 ounces boneless pork loin roast
¼ pound medium-size shrimp
1 pound bean sprouts
1½ teaspoons salt
Medium-size onion
¼ cup plus 1 tablespoon sugar
¼ cup Vietnamese fish sauce (nuoc nam) or dark soy
 sauce
1 egg
2 teaspoons vegetable oil
1 medium-size clove garlic
¼ teaspoon red pepper flakes
1 tablespoon lime juice
½ cup plus 3 tablespoons distilled white vinegar
¼ teaspoon freshly ground black pepper
Small bunch coriander
2 tablespoons dry-roasted peanuts for garnish (optional)

1. Place pork in small saucepan with 3 cups water and bring to a boil over medium-high heat. Reduce heat to medium, cover pan, and simmer 20 minutes.
2. Meanwhile, bring 6 cups water to a boil in large stockpot over high heat.
3. Pinch off legs of shrimp, several at a time, then bend back and snap off sharp, beaklike pieces of shell just above tail. Remove shell, except for tail, and discard. Using sharp paring knife, make shallow incision along back of each shrimp, exposing digestive vein. Extract vein and discard. Set shrimp aside.
4. Add bean sprouts to boiling water in large stockpot and return to a boil. Immediately turn bean sprouts into colander and refresh under cold water. Set aside to drain.
5. Bring 1 cup water and ½ teaspoon salt to a simmer in small saucepan over medium heat.
6. Meanwhile, peel and thinly slice onion.
7. Add shrimp to simmering water and cook 3 minutes.
8. Transfer drained bean sprouts to large bowl, cover, and refrigerate until 30 minutes before serving.
9. Turn shrimp into colander and set aside to drain.
10. Meanwhile, cut pork into ¼-inch-thick slices; cut slices lengthwise into thin strips. Wrap in plastic and refrigerate until 30 minutes before serving.
11. For dressing (nuoc cham), combine ¼ cup sugar, fish sauce, and ¾ cup water in small nonaluminum saucepan and bring to a boil over medium-high heat. Remove pan from heat and set aside to cool.
12. Meanwhile, for shredded egg, beat egg lightly in small bowl. Heat oil in 8-inch skillet over medium heat until hot. Pour in egg, tilting pan to coat bottom thinly and evenly. Cook 20 to 30 seconds, or just until egg sets on bottom; turn and cook another few seconds. With metal spatula, remove egg from pan; roll up jelly-roll style and cut crosswise into thin shreds. Wrap shredded egg in plastic and refrigerate until 30 minutes before serving.
13. Peel garlic and mince enough to measure ½ teaspoon.

Place in mortar and pound to a paste with pestle. Add garlic, red pepper flakes, lime juice, and 3 tablespoons vinegar to dressing. Cover pan and refrigerate until 30 minutes before serving.

14. In small nonaluminum bowl, combine remaining ½ cup vinegar, remaining 1 teaspoon salt, 1 tablespoon sugar, and black pepper. Add sliced onion, cover bowl, and refrigerate until 30 minutes before serving.

15. Thirty minutes before serving, set out all refrigerated ingredients to come to room temperature.

16. Wash and dry coriander. Set aside 3 sprigs for garnish and finely chop enough remaining coriander to measure 3 tablespoons. Coarsely chop peanuts, if using; set aside.

17. Spread bean sprouts on serving platter. Top with marinated onion slices and let stand 2 minutes.

18. Carefully drain off marinade from platter and arrange pork and shrimp over onion. Top with shredded egg and sprinkle salad with chopped coriander, peanuts if desired, and 6 tablespoons dressing. Garnish salad with coriander sprigs and serve remaining dressing separately.

Poached Chicken with Rice and Ginger Sauce

3-pound chicken, quartered
1½ cups long-grain white rice
2 medium-size cloves garlic
1-inch piece fresh ginger
¾ teaspoon salt, approximately
Pinch of sugar
Small bunch mint for garnish
Small carrot for garnish
Small cucumber for garnish
1½ teaspoons vegetable oil
Ginger Sauce (see following recipe)

1. Bring 3 quarts water to a boil in large stockpot over high heat.

2. Add chicken to boiling water, reduce heat to medium, and partially cover pot. Poach chicken 30 minutes, turning chicken pieces once during cooking time.

3. Place rice in large bowl and rinse thoroughly in cold water, rubbing rice between hands. Drain rice and repeat procedure. Turn rice into strainer and set aside to drain.

4. Remove stockpot from heat. Transfer chicken and stock to large bowl, cover, and refrigerate until 20 minutes before serving.

5. Place strainer with rice in large bowl, cover with plastic wrap, and refrigerate until 30 minutes before serving.

6. Thirty minutes before serving, remove rice, chicken, and stock from refrigerator. Peel garlic and mince enough to measure 1¾ teaspoons. Place in mortar and pound to a paste with pestle; remove from mortar and set aside. Peel and mince ginger. Place ginger and ⅛ teaspoon salt in mortar and pound with pestle.

7. Sprinkle rice with ½ teaspoon salt, sugar, 1½ teaspoons pounded garlic, and 1 tablespoon ginger-salt mixture. Stir to combine well.

8. Wash mint, carrot, and cucumber. Set aside 12 mint leaves for garnish. Peel and trim carrot and grate enough carrot to measure ½ cup. Dice enough unpeeled cucumber to measure ¼ cup. Set aside.

9. Heat oil in 3-quart saucepan over medium heat until hot. Add remaining garlic and cook until sizzling. Add rice and cook 2 minutes, stirring constantly to coat with oil.

10. Measure 1¾ cups chicken stock and add to rice; bring to a boil. Reduce heat to medium-low, cover pan, and simmer 20 minutes, or until liquid is absorbed and rice is tender.

11. Meanwhile, place chicken and remaining stock in stockpot and reheat over medium heat 15 to 20 minutes, or until hot.

12. Spread rice on serving platter. Remove chicken from stock and arrange on top of rice. Drizzle chicken with some ginger sauce and garnish with mint, carrot, and cucumber. Serve remaining sauce separately.

Ginger Sauce

1 medium-size clove garlic
1-inch piece fresh ginger
3 tablespoons sugar
½ teaspoon red pepper flakes
2 tablespoons lime juice
2 tablespoons Vietnamese fish sauce (nuoc nam) or dark
   soy sauce

1. Peel and mince garlic. Peel and mince ginger. Place garlic, ginger, and sugar in mortar and pound with pestle to a coarse paste. Transfer to small nonaluminum bowl and add red pepper, lime juice, fish sauce, and 1⅓ cups water.

2. Cover bowl and refrigerate until 30 minutes before serving.

ADDED TOUCH

For this typical Vietnamese dessert, select firm, just-ripe bananas, which hold their shape when deep fried.

Fried Bananas

3 medium-size bananas
1 cup all-purpose flour
1 tablespoon baking powder
½ cup potato starch or cornstarch
3½ to 4 cups vegetable oil
1 tablespoon confectioners' sugar

1. Peel bananas and cut crosswise into 2-inch-long pieces.

2. Combine flour, baking powder, and potato starch or cornstarch in large bowl. Add ¼ cup oil and 1½ cups water and whisk until combined.

3. Heat remaining oil in wok or large saucepan until a deep-fat thermometer registers 350 degrees. Dip bananas into batter, place gently in oil, and fry 2 minutes, turning once, or until lightly browned. Using slotted spoon, transfer bananas to paper-towel-lined platter to drain briefly.

4. To serve, place bananas on platter and dust with confectioners' sugar.

Sour Beef Salad
Sweet Pork
Broccoli with Oyster Sauce

For a taste of Thailand, prepare this meal of sour beef salad, morsels of sweet pork, and stir-fried broccoli with oyster sauce.

A primary flavoring ingredient for the sweet pork dish is tamarind water, made from the pods of the Asian tamarind tree and used as we would use lemon juice. You will find cellophane packages containing tamarind pulp and seeds, or jars of concentrated pulp, in Oriental markets. Unopened jars of pulp keep indefinitely.

The oyster sauce that flavors the broccoli is a typical Chinese condiment also used in Thai cooking. It is made from dried oysters, which are pounded and combined with soy sauce and other seasonings and then fermented. You don't have to like oysters to find the sauce appealing, since its flavor tends to enhance, not overwhelm, that of the food. Look for relatively thin oyster sauce that is light brown in color; thick, dark brown sauce is not of high quality. Once opened, the sauce should be stored in the refrigerator, where it will keep indefinitely. There is no substitute.

WHAT TO DRINK

Cold beer (especially a Chinese brand) or ale should be your first choice here. For wine, consider a dry German Riesling of the *Kabinett* class.

SHOPPING LIST AND STAPLES

1¾ pounds boneless sirloin steak, cut 1 inch thick
¾ pound boneless Boston pork butt roast or
  pork loin roast
Large bunch broccoli (about 1½ pounds)
Small head Boston lettuce
4 small fresh hot red or green chilies (optional)
1 large plus 1 medium-size yellow onion
Medium-size clove garlic
Small bunch mint
2 large limes, plus small lime if not using tamarind
¼ cup vegetable oil
6-ounce bottle Thai fish sauce (nam pla), if available
3 tablespoons dark soy sauce, plus ¼ cup if not using
  fish sauce
1 teaspoon tamarind pulp or ½ teaspoon tamarind
  concentrate, if available
9-ounce bottle oyster sauce
2 tablespoons plus 1 teaspoon sugar,
  approximately
Freshly ground black pepper

UTENSILS

Wok or large skillet
4-quart saucepan
Large saucepan
Broiler pan with rack
Large bowl
Medium-size nonaluminum bowl
2 small nonaluminum bowls
Colander
Small strainer (optional)
Measuring cups and spoons
Chef's knife
Paring knife
Wooden spoon
Citrus juicer (optional)

START-TO-FINISH STEPS

The Morning of Serving
1. Follow beef salad recipe steps 1 through 4.
2. Follow pork recipe steps 1 through 5.
3. Follow broccoli recipe steps 1 through 3.
4. Follow beef salad recipe step 5, pork recipe step 6, and broccoli recipe step 4.

Thirty Minutes Before Serving
1. Follow beef salad recipe steps 6 through 9.
2. Follow pork recipe step 7.
3. While pork is heating, follow broccoli recipe step 5.
4. Follow pork recipe step 8 and serve with broccoli and beef salad.

RECIPES

Sour Beef Salad

2 large limes
1¾ pounds boneless sirloin steak, cut 1 inch thick
¼ cup Thai fish sauce (nam pla) or dark soy sauce
1 teaspoon sugar
Large yellow onion
Small head Boston lettuce
Small bunch mint
4 small fresh hot red or green chilies (optional)

1. Preheat broiler.

2. Halve 1 lime and squeeze enough juice to measure 3 tablespoons. Reserve remaining lime for garnish.

3. Place steak on rack in broiler pan and broil 4 inches from heat 3 minutes. Meanwhile, combine lime juice, fish sauce, and sugar in small nonaluminum bowl. Cover bowl and refrigerate sauce until needed.

4. Turn steak and cook another 2 to 3 minutes (meat should be rare). Transfer steak and juices to platter and set aside to cool.

5. When cool, cover platter and refrigerate steak until 30 minutes before serving.

6. Thirty minutes before serving, set out steak and sauce to come to room temperature.

7. Meanwhile, peel onion and cut into thin rings. Wash lettuce and mint, and chilies if using, and dry with paper towels. Separate lettuce leaves, discarding any bruised or discolored leaves. Reserve 16 mint leaves for garnish. If using chilies, halve, seed, and cut crosswise into thin slices. Wash remaining lime and dry with paper towels. Cut lime into thick slices. Notch and twist each slice, if desired.

8. Transfer steak to work surface. Cut lengthwise into 2-inch-wide slices, then cut slices across the grain into ¼-inch-thick pieces. Return steak to platter with juices. If, when ready to serve, juices are still coagulated, place the platter with the steak and juices in a warm oven for a minute or two, then proceed.

9. Arrange lettuce leaves on 4 dinner plates and top with equal portions of steak, juices, and onion rings. Top each portion with 4 mint leaves, and chili slices if using. Drizzle with sauce and garnish with lime slices.

Sweet Pork

1 teaspoon tamarind pulp, or ½ teaspoon tamarind concentrate, or small lime
¾ pound boneless Boston pork butt roast or pork loin roast
Medium-size yellow onion
2 tablespoons vegetable oil
¼ teaspoon freshly ground black pepper
3 tablespoons dark soy sauce
2 tablespoons sugar

1. To prepare tamarind water, combine tamarind pulp, if using, with 2 tablespoons water in small nonaluminum bowl. Strain mixture and set aside enough to measure 1 tablespoon. Or, dissolve tamarind concentrate in 1 tablespoon hot water in small bowl. Or, halve lime and squeeze enough juice to measure 1 tablespoon; set aside.

2. Cut pork into 2-inch-long by ¼-inch-thick slices.

3. Peel onion; halve onion through stem end and slice thinly.

4. Heat oil in wok or large skillet over high heat until hot. Reduce heat to medium and, stirring constantly, add pork and pepper. Continue to stir fry 3 minutes, or until pork is no longer pink.

5. Add onion and stir fry another minute. Add soy sauce and cook 3 to 4 minutes, or until liquid is absorbed. Add sugar and tamarind water or lime juice and stir just to coat pork. Remove pan from heat and set aside to allow mixture to cool.

6. When cooled, transfer mixture to medium-size bowl, cover, and refrigerate until about 10 minutes before serving.

7. To serve, reheat pork in large saucepan over medium-low heat until hot.

8. Divide pork among 4 dinner plates.

Broccoli with Oyster Sauce

Large bunch broccoli (about 1½ pounds)
Medium-size clove garlic
2 tablespoons vegetable oil
3 tablespoons oyster sauce
Pinch of sugar

1. Bring 2 quarts water to a boil in 4-quart saucepan over high heat.

2. Meanwhile, wash broccoli and dry with paper towels. Cut tops of broccoli into small florets. Trim and discard woody stem ends, and cut stems on diagonal into ¼-inch-thick slices.

3. Add broccoli to boiling water and cook 3 minutes. Turn broccoli into colander and refresh under cold running water. Set aside to drain.

4. Transfer broccoli to large bowl, cover, and set aside at room temperature until needed.

5. Ten minutes before serving, heat wok or large skillet over high heat until hot. Meanwhile, peel and mince garlic. Reduce heat to medium, add oil and garlic, and cook garlic a few seconds, or until golden brown. Add broccoli and stir to coat with oil. Stir in oyster sauce and sugar. Cook 3 to 5 minutes, or just until broccoli is hot. Divide broccoli among 4 dinner plates.

Marie Simmons

Marie Simmons developed her taste for good food as a child. "Every Saturday I baked cakes and cookies," she remembers, "and I often helped my Italian grandmother make ravioli for holiday dinners." As an adult, Marie Simmons continues to devote a great deal of energy to refining her cooking skills and expanding her recipe knowledge. Often this requires travel, and one of her favorite destinations is Italy. The following recipes are based on some dishes she sampled in Tuscany.

In Menu 1, a pork loin roast is rubbed with rosemary and garlic, roasted early in the day, and then served at room temperature. Colorful bell peppers and onions cook along with the pork. The delicious Italian salad, called *panzanella*, contains whole-wheat bread cubes and fresh tomatoes and basil, and can be served as a first course, if desired.

An informal meal, Menu 2 calls for cubed veal in the stew, which is accompanied by fried cheese sandwiches known in Italy as *mozzarella in carrozza*, or "mozzarella in a carriage." The tart salad is a combination of three popular Italian greens.

The cook features an unusual ziti casserole in Menu 3: The ziti bakes with four different cheeses—ricotta, mozzarella, fontina, and Parmesan—rather than the traditional tomato sauce. With it, Marie Simmons offers sautéed sausages, mushrooms, and peppers and a broccoli salad prepared in the Tuscan manner (the broccoli is steamed and tossed with olive oil and lemon juice).

This sumptuous buffet becomes even more festive with the addition of flowers and handsome wineglasses. The roast loin of pork is served with bell peppers and onions and panzanella, *a marinated salad of vegetables and bread cubes.*

Panzanella
Loin of Pork with Rosemary and Garlic
Roasted Bell Peppers and Onions

A popular Florentine dish, *panzanella* depends for its success on fresh summer produce and good-quality Italian whole-wheat bread. The tomatoes must be at their flavor peak, and the basil fresh and fragrant. Leave the bread out for a day so the crust gets crisp and dry.

The pork loin roasts in less than an hour and thus remains tender and juicy. It will continue to cook after it is removed from the oven. If the day of preparation is especially hot, refrigerate the pork after it cools rather than letting it sit out. Remove it from the refrigerator in plenty of time to come to room temperature, however.

WHAT TO DRINK

A fruity white wine, such as Vernaccia di San Gimignano, is the cook's choice to go with this menu. If it is not available, try an Italian Pinot Bianco or Chardonnay.

SHOPPING LIST AND STAPLES

1¾- to 2-pound boneless pork loin roast with tenderloin
    removed, approximately 6 x 3 inches
2 pounds red, green, and/or yellow bell peppers
4 to 6 firm, ripe tomatoes (1¾ pounds total weight)
Medium-size cucumber
Small head romaine lettuce (optional)
Small bunch arugula (optional)
3 small yellow onions
Small red onion
4 medium-size cloves garlic
Small bunch each basil, mint, and flat-leaf parsley
Small lemon
6-ounce can black olives (optional)
5 tablespoons extra-virgin olive oil
3 tablespoons good-quality olive oil
2 tablespoons red wine vinegar
Small loaf day-old whole-wheat Italian bread
1 tablespoon dried rosemary
Salt and freshly ground black pepper
½ teaspoon coarsely ground black pepper, approximately

UTENSILS

Roasting pan
Roasting rack (optional)
Large shallow baking dish

Large salad bowl
Medium-size bowl
Measuring cups and spoons
Chef's knife
Paring knife
Bread knife
Wooden spoon
Metal spatula
Mortar and pestle
Meat thermometer

START-TO-FINISH STEPS

The Morning of Serving
1. Follow pork recipe steps 1 through 3 and peppers recipe steps 1 through 3.
2. While pork and peppers are roasting, follow panzanella recipe steps 1 through 5.
3. Follow peppers recipe step 4 and pork recipe step 4.
4. Follow peppers recipe step 5.

Ten Minutes Before Serving
1. Follow pork recipe step 5.
2. Follow panzanella recipe step 6, pork recipe step 6, and serve with peppers.

RECIPES

Panzanella

Small loaf day-old whole-wheat Italian bread
Medium-size cucumber
Small red onion
Small bunch basil
4 to 6 firm, ripe tomatoes (1¾ pounds total weight)
5 tablespoons extra-virgin olive oil
2 tablespoons red wine vinegar
Salt
¼ teaspoon coarsely ground pepper, approximately
Small head romaine lettuce (optional)

1. Cut bread into eight ½-inch-thick slices. Cut slices into enough ½-inch cubes to measure 2 cups. Place bread cubes in medium-size bowl and add cold water to cover. Let stand about 5 minutes.
2. Meanwhile, wash and dry cucumber. Halve cucumber lengthwise. Trim ends, scrape out seeds with teaspoon,

and discard seeds. Cut enough cucumber into ¼-inch dice to measure 1½ cups. Peel onion; coarsely chop enough onion to measure ¾ cup.

3. Drain bread, gently squeezing out moisture with hands so cubes retain shape.

4. Wash and dry basil. Coarsely chop enough basil leaves to measure 3 tablespoons. Wash, dry, and core tomatoes. Cut tomatoes into 1-inch pieces.

5. In large salad bowl, mix bread, cucumber, onion, basil, tomatoes, 4 tablespoons olive oil, 1 tablespoon vinegar, 1 teaspoon salt, and ¼ teaspoon pepper. Cover, and let stand at room temperature at least 2 hours, or until just before serving.

6. To serve, add remaining olive oil and vinegar, and additional salt and pepper to taste to salad. Serve salad directly from salad bowl, or line platter with romaine leaves and spoon salad onto center of leaves.

Loin of Pork with Rosemary and Garlic

3 medium-size cloves garlic
1 tablespoon dried rosemary
1 teaspoon salt
¼ teaspoon freshly ground black pepper
1¾- to 2-pound boneless pork loin roast with tenderloin removed, approximately 6 x 3 inches
Small bunch arugula for garnish (optional)
Black olives for garnish (optional)

1. Preheat oven to 400 degrees.
2. Meanwhile, peel and coarsely chop garlic. Crush garlic, rosemary, salt, and pepper together in mortar with pestle until mixture is paste-like. Rub mixture over entire surface of pork. Place pork in roasting pan, on rack if desired.
3. Roast on middle rack of oven 50 to 55 minutes, or until meat thermometer registers 150 degrees.
4. Cover pork loosely and let stand at room temperature until ready to serve.
5. Ten minutes before serving, wash arugula and drain olives, if using.
6. To serve, place pork on carving board or platter and slice thinly. Garnish with arugula and olives if desired.

Roasted Bell Peppers and Onions

Medium-size clove garlic
2 pounds red, green, and/or yellow bell peppers
3 small yellow onions
3 tablespoons good-quality olive oil
½ teaspoon salt
⅛ teaspoon coarsely ground black pepper
Small bunch flat-leaf parsley
Small bunch mint
Small lemon

1. Peel and halve garlic. Rub inside surface of large shallow baking dish with cut sides of garlic; leave garlic in dish.
2. Wash and dry peppers. Quarter peppers, discarding core and seeds. Peel onions and cut in half through stem end. Combine peppers and onions in baking dish. Drizzle with oil; sprinkle with salt and pepper.
3. Roast vegetables on top rack of preheated 400-degree oven, turning occasionally with spatula, about 45 minutes, or until browned and tender.
4. Turn peppers and onions into serving bowl.
5. Wash parsley and mint and pat dry with paper towels. Finely chop enough parsley to measure 2 tablespoons and enough mint to measure 1 teaspoon. Sprinkle parsley and mint over roasted peppers. Halve lemon and squeeze enough juice to measure 1 tablespoon. Drizzle juice over peppers and toss gently. Cover bowl and let peppers and onions stand at room temperature until ready to serve.

ADDED TOUCH

This refreshing ice is one of the most popular Italian hot-weather desserts and should be made with only the highest-quality freshly ground espresso.

Espresso Granita with Cream

⅔ cup finely ground espresso
1 cup sugar
Small lemon
1 cup heavy cream, well chilled
Unsweetened cocoa powder

1. Place coffee in paper coffee filter or in fine sieve lined with dampened paper towel. Slowly pour 3 cups boiling water over coffee into bowl; discard grounds.
2. Add sugar to coffee and stir about 2 minutes, or until sugar is completely dissolved.
3. With paring knife, remove 1 by ½-inch strip of lemon rind; reserve lemon for another use. Twist rind over coffee to release oils; add rind to coffee.
4. Refrigerate coffee mixture at least 2 hours, or until very cold.
5. Pour cold coffee mixture into shallow 8-inch square metal pan. Freeze about 2 hours, or until edges are firm and center is still slushy.
6. Stir well with whisk, mixing firm edges with slushy center. Return to freezer. Place whisk and medium-size bowl in freezer to chill 1 hour.
7. After 1 hour, scrape partially frozen granita into chilled bowl and whisk vigorously with chilled whisk to break up ice crystals. Transfer to plastic container, cover tightly, and freeze at least 3 hours, or overnight.
8. One hour before serving, place medium-size bowl, beaters, and 4 goblets or dessert dishes in freezer to chill.
9. To serve, whip cream in chilled bowl until soft peaks form. Scrape granita into chilled goblets or dessert dishes and top with a dollop of whipped cream. Dust top of granita with some cocoa powder sifted through sieve.

LEFTOVER SUGGESTION

Combine leftover pork and peppers in a hearty and delicious hero sandwich.

Veal Stew
Mozzarella in Carrozza
Arugula, Chicory, and Escarole Salad

Crisp deep-fried cheese sandwiches are melt-in-the-mouth accompaniments for a rich veal stew and tossed green salad.

The deep-fried mozzarella sandwiches make a delicious appetizer, snack, or complement to a salad or main course, as here. Be sure to use a firm-textured bread that will not disintegrate when dipped into the egg-milk mixture. Dip the sandwiches into the liquid just long enough for the bread to be uniformly moistened. The best cheese for this sandwich is whole-milk mozzarella because it melts more smoothly and has a richer taste than its skim-milk counterpart.

If the weather is especially hot, refrigerate the stew, but remember to remove it from the refrigerator in plenty of time to come to room temperature.

WHAT TO DRINK

A crisp Pinot Grigio or Verdicchio, or a Sicilian white wine, would be good in the stew and for drinking with dinner. A light red wine, such as an Italian Barbera or a California Gamay Beaujolais, is also excellent with veal.

SHOPPING LIST AND STAPLES

2 pounds veal stew meat, trimmed of fat and gristle and cut into 1-inch cubes

2 ounces pancetta or slab bacon
Small bunch celery with leaves
Small head chicory
Small head escarole
Small bunch arugula
Medium-size onion
2 medium-size cloves garlic
Small bunch flat-leaf parsley
2 eggs
2 tablespoons milk
½ pound whole-milk mozzarella cheese, preferably
    freshly made
14½-ounce can whole Italian plum tomatoes
⅓ cup extra-virgin olive oil
¼ cup good-quality olive oil
1 cup vegetable oil and 1 cup good-quality olive oil, or 2
    cups vegetable oil, approximately
1 tablespoon plus 2 teaspoons balsamic vinegar or other
    aged red wine vinegar
¼ cup all-purpose flour
Long thin loaf whole-wheat or white Italian bread
Salt
Freshly ground black pepper
1 bay leaf
½ cup dry white wine

UTENSILS

2 large heavy-gauge skillets, one with cover
Small saucepan (optional)
Large bowl
2 small bowls
Salad spinner (optional)
Strainer
Measuring cups and spoons
Chef's knife
Paring knife
Bread knife
Wooden spoon
Slotted spatula
Small jar with tight-fitting lid
Wooden toothpicks

START-TO-FINISH STEPS

The Morning of Serving
1. Follow stew recipe steps 1 through 6.
2. While stew is cooking, follow mozzarella recipe step 1
and salad recipe steps 1 and 2.
3. Follow stew recipe step 7.

About Fifteen Minutes Before Serving
1. Follow mozzarella recipe steps 2 and 3 and stew recipe
steps 8 and 9.
2. While stew is reheating, follow salad recipe step 3 and
mozzarella recipe step 4.
3. Follow salad recipe step 4, stew recipe steps 10 and 11,
mozzarella recipe step 5, and serve.

RECIPES

Veal Stew

2 ounces pancetta or slab bacon
Medium-size onion
Medium-size clove garlic
Medium-size stalk celery with leaves
¼ cup good-quality olive oil
1 bay leaf
14½-ounce can whole Italian plum tomatoes
2 pounds veal stew meat, trimmed of fat and gristle and
    cut into 1-inch cubes
½ cup dry white wine
Small bunch flat-leaf parsley
½ teaspoon salt
¼ teaspoon freshly ground black pepper

1. Cut pancetta or slab bacon into ¼-inch dice. If using
slab bacon, blanch in 2 cups boiling water in small saucepan 5 minutes to remove some of smoky flavor; turn into
strainer and drain well.
2. Peel onion and cut into ¼-inch pieces. Peel and mince
garlic. Trim celery stalk and cut into ¼-inch dice; coarsely
chop celery leaves.
3. In large heavy-gauge skillet, sauté pancetta or slab
bacon in oil over medium-high heat about 4 minutes, or
until lightly browned.
4. Stir in onion, garlic, celery, and bay leaf, cover pan, and
reduce heat to very low. Cook 15 minutes, stirring frequently; do not brown.
5. Meanwhile, drain tomatoes in strainer set over small
bowl. Reserve juice. Break up tomatoes with hands,
squeezing out and discarding all seeds.
6. Add tomatoes, tomato juice, veal, and wine to cooked
onions. Increase heat to high and cook, stirring, until
liquid comes to a boil. Reduce heat to low and cook stew,
covered, 45 minutes.
7. Remove stew from heat and let stand, covered, at room
temperature until about 15 minutes before serving.
8. About 15 minutes before serving, reheat stew over high
heat, uncovered, stirring often, until veal is heated
through and juices are reduced.
9. Meanwhile, wash parsley and pat dry with paper towels. Coarsely chop enough parsley to measure 1 tablespoon.
10. Just before serving, stir 2 teaspoons parsley into stew.
Add salt and pepper and cook, stirring, 1 minute. Remove
bay leaf.
11. Divide stew among 4 dinner plates, sprinkle with remaining teaspoon parsley, and serve.

Mozzarella in Carrozza

Long thin loaf whole-wheat or white Italian bread
½ pound whole-milk mozzarella cheese, preferably
    freshly made
1 cup vegetable oil and 1 cup good-quality olive oil, or 2
    cups vegetable oil, approximately

¼ cup all-purpose flour
2 eggs
2 tablespoons milk

1. Cut bread into sixteen ½-inch-thick slices. Cut mozzarella into eight ¼-inch-thick slices. Place 1 slice of cheese between each 2 slices of bread. Skewer each sandwich with toothpick inserted at an angle so that only about ⅛ inch of wood extends from either side of sandwich. Place sandwiches on platter, cover loosely with plastic wrap, and set aside at room temperature until needed.
2. About 15 minutes before serving, pour 1 inch of oil into large heavy-gauge skillet. Heat over medium-high heat about 5 minutes, or until crust of bread dropped into oil immediately begins to sizzle and brown. Meanwhile, place flour on plate. Place eggs and milk in small bowl and beat with fork to combine; pour mixture into shallow platter.
3. Preheat oven to 200 degrees.
4. When oil is hot, quickly dust sandwiches with flour and dip into egg-milk mixture to coat. Fry sandwiches in oil, 2 or 3 at a time, about 1 minute per side, turning as they begin to brown. Using slotted spatula, lift from hot oil; let excess oil drip off. Place on ovenproof platter and keep warm in oven. Repeat with remaining sandwiches.
5. Remove sandwiches from oven, remove toothpicks, and serve at once.

Arugula, Chicory, and Escarole Salad

Small bunch arugula
Small head chicory
Small head escarole
⅓ cup extra-virgin olive oil
1 tablespoon plus 2 teaspoons balsamic vinegar or other
   aged red wine vinegar
½ teaspoon salt
⅛ teaspoon freshly ground black pepper
Medium-size clove garlic

1. Carefully wash arugula and dry in salad spinner or with paper towels. Snap off and discard tough ends of stems, leaving about 2 inches of tender stem attached to leaves. You should have about 2 cups leaves. Rinse and dry chicory and escarole; tear enough into 2-inch pieces to measure about 2 cups each. Wrap greens in kitchen towel, place in plastic bag, and refrigerate until ready to use.
2. Combine oil, vinegar, salt, and pepper in jar with tight-fitting lid. Set aside at room temperature until needed.

3. Just before serving, peel garlic and cut in half. Lightly rub inside of large bowl with cut sides of garlic; discard garlic. Place arugula, chicory, and escarole in bowl. Shake dressing to recombine and pour over greens. Toss well.
4. Divide salad among 4 dinner or salad plates.

Arugula

ADDED TOUCH

This version of *tartufi* (Italian for "truffles") resembles a dessert the cook enjoyed in a restaurant in Rome.

Tartufi

1 pint good-quality chocolate ice cream
4 brandied cherries
4 ounces semisweet chocolate
4 tablespoons unsalted butter
½ cup heavy cream, well chilled

1. Place small wire rack in metal pie plate or 8-inch square baking pan and place in freezer 10 minutes.
2. Scoop out 4 well-rounded balls of ice cream and place on chilled rack. Freeze about 1 hour, or until very firm.
3. Remove ice cream balls from freezer and push 1 cherry into underside of each. Return to freezer.
4. In small saucepan, melt chocolate and butter over very low heat, stirring constantly, about 3 minutes, or until completely melted. Remove pan from heat and, using rubber spatula, scrape chocolate into small shallow bowl. Let chocolate cool a few minutes; do not let cool too long or mixture will harden.
5. Remove pan with ice cream balls from freezer, and pour chocolate evenly over balls to coat. Immediately return pan with ice cream to freezer and freeze at least 1 hour longer. Place medium-size bowl and beaters in freezer to chill.
6. Just before serving, whip cream in chilled bowl until soft peaks form. Divide cream evenly among 4 dessert bowls and place 1 tartufo in the center of each. Serve at once.

Ziti with Four Cheeses
Sautéed Sweet Sausage, Mushrooms, and Bell Peppers
Broccoli Salad

Serve the ziti before the entrée, Italian style, or offer it with the sautéed sausages, mushrooms, and peppers and the broccoli salad.

The sausage, mushroom, and pepper sauté is simple to prepare and is sparked by the last-minute addition of fresh herbs. If you cannot buy all the herbs fresh, try this trick: Place the fresh parsley on a cutting board and add the dried mint, thyme, and/or basil. Using a chef's knife, chop all the herbs together until the parsley is finely minced and the dried herbs are moistened by the fresh parsley juice. This allows the dried herbs to release their maximum flavor—far more than when added in their dry form.

WHAT TO DRINK

A young Chianti Classico is a good choice here. Or, try a simple Zinfandel, mineral water, or seltzer.

SHOPPING LIST AND STAPLES

1½ pounds sweet Italian link sausage (6 or 7 large links)
¾ pound medium-size fresh mushrooms
Large bunch broccoli (about 1½ pounds)
Small red bell pepper
Small bunch fresh mint, or 1 teaspoon dried
Small bunch fresh basil, or 1 teaspoon dried
Small bunch fresh thyme, or ½ teaspoon dried
Small bunch flat-leaf parsley
Large lemon
1 egg
2 tablespoons unsalted butter
15-ounce container whole-milk ricotta cheese
½ pound whole-milk mozzarella cheese, preferably freshly made
¼ pound fontina or Bel Paese cheese
2 ounces Parmesan cheese
½ cup good-quality olive oil
¾ pound ziti
Ground nutmeg
Salt
Freshly ground black pepper

UTENSILS

Food processor (optional)
Large skillet with cover

71

2 large saucepans with covers
Collapsible vegetable steamer
Medium-size shallow baking dish
2 medium-size bowls
Small bowl
Colander
Measuring cups and spoons
Chef's knife
Paring knife
Wooden spoon
Metal spatula
Grater
Small jar with tight-fitting lid

START-TO-FINISH STEPS

The Day Before or the Morning of Serving

1. Follow ziti recipe step 1. Wash parsley and pat dry with paper towels. Finely chop enough parsley to measure 2 tablespoons for ziti recipe and refrigerate remaining parsley for sausage recipe.
2. Follow ziti recipe steps 2 and 3.
3. While ziti is cooking, follow broccoli recipe step 1.
4. Follow ziti recipe step 4 and broccoli recipe step 2.
5. While broccoli is cooking, follow sausage recipe step 1.
6. While sausage is cooking, follow broccoli recipe step 3 and ziti recipe steps 5 and 6.
7. Follow sausage recipe step 2 and broccoli recipe steps 4 and 5.

Thirty Minutes Before Serving

1. Follow sausage recipe step 3, broccoli recipe step 6, and ziti recipe steps 7 and 8.
2. While ziti is baking, follow sausage recipe steps 4 and 5.
3. Ten minutes before ziti is done, follow broccoli recipe step 7 and sausage recipe steps 6 and 7.
4. Follow broccoli recipe step 8, ziti recipe step 9, and serve with sausage.

RECIPES

Ziti with Four Cheeses

½ pound whole-milk mozzarella cheese, preferably freshly made
¼ pound fontina or Bel Paese cheese
2 ounces Parmesan cheese

¾ pound ziti (about 5 cups uncooked)
Salt
15-ounce container whole-milk ricotta cheese
1 egg
2 tablespoons finely chopped flat-leaf parsley
Pinch of ground nutmeg
¼ teaspoon freshly ground black pepper

1. In large saucepan, bring 3 quarts water to a boil over high heat.
2. Using food processor or grater, coarsely shred enough mozzarella to measure 2 cups and enough fontina or Bel Paese to measure 1 cup. Grate enough Parmesan to measure ½ cup. Set aside.
3. When water boils, stir in ziti and 1 tablespoon salt. Cover and cook ziti over high heat until water returns to a full rolling boil. Uncover and cook ziti, stirring occasionally, another 8 minutes, or just until *al dente*.
4. Drain ziti in colander and return to pan; set aside.
5. In small bowl, beat ricotta and egg. Add ricotta mixture, mozzarella, fontina or Bel Paese, Parmesan, parsley, nutmeg, and pepper to ziti and stir to combine well.
6. Generously butter medium-size shallow baking dish. Spoon ziti mixture into dish; cover with plastic wrap and refrigerate until 30 minutes before serving.
7. Thirty minutes before serving, preheat oven to 375 degrees.
8. Uncover ziti and bake 20 to 25 minutes, or until top begins to brown and center is heated through.
9. Divide ziti among 4 plates and serve.

Sautéed Sweet Sausage, Mushrooms, and Bell Peppers

1½ pounds sweet Italian link sausage (6 or 7 large links)
¾ pound medium-size fresh mushrooms
Small bunch flat-leaf parsley, washed
Small bunch fresh mint, or 1 teaspoon dried
Small bunch fresh basil, or 1 teaspoon dried
Small bunch fresh thyme, or ½ teaspoon dried
Small red bell pepper
2 tablespoons good-quality olive oil
2 tablespoons unsalted butter
½ teaspoon salt
⅛ teaspoon freshly ground black pepper

1. Slit sausage casings lengthwise and peel off. In large

72

skillet, sauté sausage over low heat about 2 minutes, stirring to break up meat. Cover skillet and cook about 10 minutes, or until meat loses its pink color.

2. Uncover skillet and drain off all fat. Sauté sausage over medium heat, stirring to break up any large clumps, another 5 minutes, or until evenly browned. Transfer sausage to medium-size bowl, cover, and refrigerate until 30 minutes before serving.

3. Thirty minutes before serving, set sausage out to come to room temperature.

4. Wipe mushrooms with damp paper towels and cut into ¼-inch-thick slices; you should have about 5 cups. Finely chop enough parsley to measure 3 tablespoons; set aside. If using other fresh herbs, wash and pat dry with paper towels. Finely chop enough mint and basil to measure 1 tablespoon each. Finely chop enough thyme to measure 1½ teaspoons; set aside.

5. Wash and dry bell pepper. Halve, core, seed, and cut pepper into ¼-inch dice.

6. Heat oil and butter in large skillet over medium heat. When butter melts and foam subsides, increase heat to high and add mushrooms. Sauté, stirring constantly, about 5 minutes, or until liquid has evaporated and mushrooms have begun to brown.

7. Stir in sausage and sauté about 3 minutes, or until heated through. Stir in parsley, fresh or dried herbs, and bell pepper, and sauté, stirring constantly, 1 minute. Season with salt and pepper and divide among 4 dinner plates.

Broccoli Salad

Large bunch broccoli (about 1½ pounds)
Large lemon
¼ cup plus 2 tablespoons good-quality olive oil
½ teaspoon salt
Freshly ground black pepper

1. Wash broccoli and cut into florets. Peel stalks if tough, halve if large, and cut stalks into 2-inch pieces.

2. In large saucepan fitted with vegetable steamer, bring 1 inch water to a boil over high heat. Place broccoli in steamer, cover, and steam 5 to 8 minutes, or until tender.

3. Turn broccoli into colander and refresh under cold running water. Drain well, turn into medium-size bowl, and refrigerate until ready to serve.

4. Wash lemon and grate enough zest from one half to measure ½ teaspoon. Halve lemon and squeeze enough juice from zested half to measure 2 tablespoons; wrap

remaining half in plastic and refrigerate until needed for garnish.

5. Combine lemon juice, lemon zest, olive oil, salt, and pepper to taste in small jar with tight-fitting lid; shake well and refrigerate until needed.

6. Thirty minutes before serving, set out broccoli and dressing to come to room temperature.

7. Just before serving, cut reserved lemon half into 4 wedges. Shake dressing to recombine and pour over broccoli. Toss gently to coat with dressing.

8. Divide broccoli among 4 dinner or salad plates and garnish each serving with a lemon wedge.

ADDED TOUCH

Italians love fresh or cooked fruit for dessert. This offering of oranges poached in a white wine syrup makes a refreshing conclusion to a rich meal.

Oranges Poached in White Wine

1 cup fruity white wine, such as Pinot Grigio, Vernaccia di San Gimignano, or Chardonnay
1 cup sugar
4 navel oranges
Small bunch mint (optional)

1. Combine wine, sugar, and 2 cups water in medium-size nonaluminum saucepan. Bring to a boil over medium heat and cook, stirring, about 1 minute, or until sugar dissolves. Simmer, uncovered, 10 minutes.

2. Meanwhile, wash and dry oranges. Using vegetable peeler, remove three 2 by 2½-inch strips of orange peel. Cut strips into very thin julienne; set aside. Using sharp knife, remove peel and pith from oranges.

3. Carefully submerge oranges in simmering syrup. Add julienned peel. Cover pan and simmer over low heat 20 minutes.

4. Remove pan from heat. Transfer oranges, syrup, and zest to heatproof bowl and let cool to room temperature. Refrigerate at least 3 hours, or until well chilled.

5. Just before serving, wash and dry mint, if using, and set aside 4 sprigs for garnish.

6. To serve, cut each orange crosswise into 4 slices and reassemble. Place each orange in shallow bowl. Ladle some syrup and julienned peel over and around each orange. Serve chilled or at room temperature, garnished with mint sprigs, if desired.

Penelope Casas

According to Penelope Casas, who made her first visit to Spain more than 20 years ago, Spanish cooking varies from region to region, but certain staples—olive oil, garlic, onions, and parsley—are used routinely throughout the country. "It is hard to imagine a Spanish meal that does not include at least one of these ingredients," she says.

Pork, perhaps the most commonly eaten meat in Spain, is the highlight of Menu 1. The cook marinates pork chops overnight in olive oil, wine, and herbs, then broils them just before serving. With the chops, she serves mushrooms in green sauce. The color and distinctive flavor of the sauce come from the large quantity of parsley used in the recipe.

Menu 2 begins with an unusual soup—a purée of zucchini and lettuce flavored with onion and mellowed with heavy cream, which can be served chilled or hot to suit the season. Codfish steaks topped with vegetables and ham bake in foil packets while you enjoy the first course.

All four Spanish staples come into play in the entrée of Menu 3, in which chicken parts are browned in olive oil and butter, then simmered in a distinctive Spanish sauce containing ground almonds and pine nuts, white wine, parsley, garlic, and onions. With the chicken, Penelope Casas offers a substantial baked rice casserole and a composed vegetable salad.

Fanciful tableware enlivens this Spanish meal of broiled pork chops and whole mushrooms simmered briefly in green sauce. The potatoes and onions are sprinkled with parsley for color.

75

Marinated Broiled Pork Chops
Mushrooms in Green Sauce
Skillet Potatoes and Onions

Pork lends itself to marinating in olive oil, wine, and seasonings, and for this recipe should remain in the marinade at least 12 hours. Here, saffron adds its unique color and flavor. The world's costliest spice, saffron is available powdered but is sold more often as whole threads, which the cook prefers. A little saffron goes a long way: A quarter ounce should last for many months of cooking.

WHAT TO DRINK

The cook recommends a good, robust Spanish red wine with this menu. Look for one from either Rioja or the Penedès region. A four- or five-year-old Italian Chianti Classico or California Zinfandel would also be good.

SHOPPING LIST AND STAPLES

Four 1-inch-thick loin pork chops (about 2½ pounds total weight), trimmed of all fat
¾ pound small to medium-size white mushrooms
3 medium-size Idaho or all-purpose potatoes (about 1¼ pounds total weight)
Small bunch red radishes (optional)
2 medium-size yellow onions (about 1 pound total weight)
6 medium-size cloves garlic
Large bunch parsley
¾ cup chicken stock, preferably homemade (see page 10), or canned
1 cup good-quality olive oil, approximately
1½ tablespoons all-purpose flour
Large pinch of saffron threads
1¾ teaspoons dried thyme
¾ teaspoon dried oregano
Salt and freshly ground pepper
½ cup dry white wine, approximately

UTENSILS

Large ovenproof skillet with cover
Medium-size nonaluminum skillet
Broiler pan with rack
Large shallow nonaluminum bowl
3 small bowls
Measuring cups and spoons
Chef's knife
Paring knife

Wooden spoon
Slotted spoon
Wide metal spatula
Whisk
Basting brush

START-TO-FINISH STEPS

The Day Before Serving

1. Peel garlic. Mince 4 cloves for pork chops recipe and 2 cloves for mushrooms recipe. Peel onions. Cut 4 thin slices for pork chops recipe and set aside. Thinly slice enough remaining onions to measure ½ cup for potatoes recipe. Finely chop enough remaining onions to measure 2 tablespoons for mushrooms recipe. Wash and dry parsley. Reserve 8 sprigs. Finely chop enough parsley to measure 2 tablespoons for pork chops recipe. Refrigerate remaining parsley for mushrooms recipe.
2. Follow pork chops recipe steps 1 and 2 and potatoes recipe steps 1 and 2.
3. While potatoes are cooking, follow mushrooms recipe steps 1 through 3.
4. Follow potatoes recipe steps 3 and 4.

Thirty Minutes Before Serving

1. Follow potatoes recipe step 5, pork chops recipe step 3, and mushrooms recipe steps 4 through 6.
2. Follow pork chops recipe steps 4 through 6.
3. While pork chops are broiling, follow potatoes recipe steps 6 and 7. (If using combination oven-broiler, place potatoes on lower rack.)
4. Follow pork chops recipe step 7, potatoes recipe step 8, mushrooms recipe step 7, and serve.

RECIPES

Marinated Broiled Pork Chops

½ cup good-quality olive oil
3 tablespoons dry white wine
4 medium-size cloves garlic, minced
2 tablespoons finely chopped parsley, plus 4 sprigs for garnish
Large pinch of saffron threads
¾ teaspoon each dried thyme and oregano
Salt and freshly ground pepper
Four 1-inch-thick loin pork chops (about 2½ pounds total weight), trimmed of all fat

4 thin slices onion
Four red radishes for garnish (optional)

1. In small bowl, whisk together oil and wine. Add garlic, chopped parsley, saffron, thyme, oregano, and salt and pepper to taste, and whisk to combine.
2. Pour marinade into large shallow nonaluminum bowl. Add chops in one layer, turn to coat with marinade, and scatter onion slices on top. Cover tightly with foil and marinate in refrigerator 12 to 24 hours, turning chops occasionally.
3. Thirty minutes before serving, preheat broiler.
4. Remove chops from marinade and place on rack in broiler pan; brush chops with marinade. Broil 4 to 5 inches from heat 4 minutes. Brush chops with marinade and broil another 4 minutes.
5. Meanwhile, if using radishes for garnish, wash, trim, and cut into mushroom shape, if desired (see page 8).
6. Turn chops, brush with marinade, and continue broiling another 5 minutes. Brush with marinade, lay onion slices on top, and broil chops another 3 to 5 minutes, or until chops are cooked through but still juicy.
7. Divide chops among 4 dinner plates and spoon pan juices over them. Garnish each plate with a parsley sprig, and a radish mushroom if desired.

Mushrooms in Green Sauce

¾ pound small to medium-size white mushrooms
3 tablespoons good-quality olive oil
2 tablespoons finely chopped onion
2 medium-size cloves garlic, minced
1½ tablespoons all-purpose flour
¼ cup dry white wine
¾ cup chicken stock
Salt and freshly ground pepper
Large bunch parsley, washed and dried

1. Wipe mushrooms clean with damp paper towels, trim stems, and halve mushrooms if large; set aside.
2. In medium-size nonaluminum skillet, heat 2 tablespoons oil over high heat until oil reaches smoking point. Add mushrooms and sauté, stirring constantly, 2 to 3 minutes, or until mushrooms are browned and softened but have not yet released their liquid. Turn off heat. With slotted spoon, transfer mushrooms to small bowl. Cover and refrigerate until 30 minutes before serving.
3. When skillet has cooled slightly, heat remaining tablespoon oil over medium heat. Add onion and sauté 2 min-

utes, or until wilted but not colored. Stir in garlic. Add flour and cook, stirring constantly, 1 minute. Gradually stir in wine and stock. Add salt and pepper to taste and cook 4 to 5 minutes, or until sauce is thickened and smooth. Remove sauce from heat, turn into small bowl, cover, and refrigerate until 30 minutes before serving.
4. Thirty minutes before serving, reheat sauce in skillet over medium-low heat.
5. Meanwhile, finely chop enough parsley to measure ½ cup.
6. Add parsley and mushrooms to sauce, stir to combine, and simmer just until mushrooms are heated through. Remove skillet from heat and let mushrooms stand at room temperature until ready to serve.
7. To serve, divide mushrooms among 4 dinner plates.

Skillet Potatoes and Onions

3 medium-size Idaho or all-purpose potatoes (about 1¼ pounds total weight)
3 tablespoons good-quality olive oil
Salt and freshly ground black pepper
1 teaspoon dried thyme
½ cup thinly sliced onions
4 sprigs parsley

1. Peel potatoes and cut into ⅛-inch-thick slices.
2. In large ovenproof skillet, heat oil over medium-high heat. Add 1 layer of potatoes and sprinkle with some salt, pepper, and thyme. Continue layering potatoes with seasonings until half of potatoes are used. Scatter sliced onions over potatoes. Continue layering potatoes and seasonings until all potatoes are used. Cook potatoes another 2 to 3 minutes, or until bottom layer is lightly browned. Using wide metal spatula, lift and turn potatoes. Cover skillet and reduce heat to medium-low. Cook potatoes about 15 minutes, or until tender.
3. Remove skillet from heat and set potatoes aside to come to room temperature.
4. Once cooled, cover skillet and refrigerate until 30 minutes before serving.
5. Thirty minutes before serving, remove skillet from refrigerator and uncover.
6. Place skillet on top rack of preheated 500-degree oven and bake potatoes 8 minutes, or until heated through.
7. Meanwhile, finely chop parsley sprigs.
8. Turn potatoes, bottom-layer up, onto serving platter, sprinkle with parsley, and serve.

Chilled Zucchini and Lettuce Soup
Codfish Steaks with Julienned Vegetables

Paired with a first course of creamy vegetable soup, the ample entrée of codfish steak topped with julienned vegetables and ham will surely satisfy even the hungriest guest. Chilled white wine is the perfect beverage.

Although often associated with New England cookery, cod is popular in Spain, where it turns up in many different guises. Cod has lean, firm, mild-tasting flesh that flakes easily when cooked. Fresh cod is available at most supermarkets and fish dealers, where it is sold whole, dressed, or as fillets or steaks. For this recipe you need steaks. The fish can be made the morning of serving, then wrapped in foil and refrigerated until ready to bake.

WHAT TO DRINK

A Spanish wine is in order here: Select a firm, dry white from Rioja or the Penedès.

SHOPPING LIST AND STAPLES

1 ounce cured ham, such as prosciutto
Four 1-inch-thick codfish, halibut, or monkfish steaks (about 2 pounds total weight)
8 medium-size white mushrooms (about 3 ounces total weight)
¼ pound green beans
3 medium-size zucchini (about 1¼ pounds total weight)
Small head romaine lettuce
Large bunch scallions
Small bunch celery
Medium-size carrot
1 medium-size onion plus 1 small onion
Small bunch parsley
1 pint heavy cream
4 tablespoons unsalted butter
2⅔ cups chicken stock, preferably homemade (see page 10), or canned
2 tablespoons good-quality olive oil
1 teaspoon Dijon mustard
Dash of hot pepper sauce
¾ teaspoon dried thyme
1 bay leaf
Freshly grated nutmeg
Salt and freshly ground pepper
¼ cup dry (fino) Spanish sherry

UTENSILS

Food processor or blender
Large nonaluminum skillet with cover

17 x 11-inch baking sheet
Medium-size bowl
2 small bowls
Salad spinner (optional)
Strainer
Measuring cups and spoons
Chef's knife
Paring knife
Wooden spoon
Slotted spatula
Rubber spatula
Ladle
Vegetable peeler (optional)

START-TO-FINISH STEPS

The Day Before or the Morning of Serving

1. Follow soup recipe steps 1 through 3.
2. Follow fish recipe steps 1 through 9.

Twenty Minutes Before Serving

1. Follow fish recipe steps 10 and 11.
2. While fish is baking, follow soup recipe step 4 and serve as first course.
3. Follow fish recipe step 12 and serve.

RECIPES

Chilled Zucchini and Lettuce Soup

Medium-size onion
3 medium-size scallions
3 medium-size zucchini (about 1¼ pounds
    total weight)
Small head romaine lettuce
2 tablespoons unsalted butter
2 tablespoons good-quality olive oil
¼ teaspoon dried thyme
Freshly grated nutmeg
2⅔ cups chicken stock
¼ cup plus 1 tablespoon heavy cream
Salt
Freshly ground pepper

1. Peel and trim onion. Wash and trim scallions and zucchini. Wash romaine and dry in salad spinner or with paper towels; discard any bruised or discolored leaves.

Using food processor or chef's knife, coarsely chop enough onion to measure 1½ cups, enough scallions to measure ⅓ cup, enough zucchini to measure 4 cups, and enough romaine leaves to measure 2 cups.
2. In large skillet, melt butter in oil over medium heat. Add onion and scallions and sauté 2 minutes, or until onion wilts. Add lettuce and zucchini and sauté 2 to 3 minutes, or until zucchini softens.
3. Turn mixture into food processor or blender. Add thyme and a generous pinch of nutmeg and purée until mixture is as smooth as possible. With machine running, gradually add stock and process until smooth. Slowly add cream and process until incorporated. Strain soup into medium-size bowl, season with salt and pepper to taste, and cover. Refrigerate at least 3 hours.
4. To serve, ladle soup into individual bowls.

Codfish Steaks with Julienned Vegetables

Small onion
Medium-size stalk celery
2 sprigs parsley
½ teaspoon dried thyme
1 bay leaf
Salt
Freshly ground pepper
Medium-size carrot
5 medium-size scallions
¼ pound green beans
8 medium-size white mushrooms (about 3 ounces
    total weight)
2 tablespoons unsalted butter
1 cup heavy cream
1 teaspoon Dijon mustard
¼ cup dry (fino) Spanish sherry
Dash of hot pepper sauce
Four 1-inch-thick codfish, halibut, or monkfish steaks
    (about 2 pounds total weight)
1 ounce cured ham, such as prosciutto

1. Peel and halve onion. Cut celery stalk into 3 pieces.
2. In large nonaluminum skillet, combine ¾ cup water with onion, celery, parsley, thyme, bay leaf, and salt and pepper to taste. Bring to a boil over high heat, reduce heat to medium, and simmer, covered, 7 minutes.
3. Meanwhile, trim and peel carrot. Wash and trim scallions and green beans. Cut enough carrot, scallions, and

green beans into 2-inch lengths to measure about ½ cup each, then cut pieces lengthwise into julienne. Wipe mushrooms clean with damp paper towel; trim stems and cut mushrooms into slices.

4. Add carrot and green beans to cooking liquid, cover, and cook 3 to 5 minutes, or until crisp-tender. If necessary, add ¼ cup additional water.

5. Turn vegetables into strainer set over small bowl; reserve broth. Measure broth and, if necessary, add water to make ½ cup.

6. Wipe skillet with paper towel. Melt butter in skillet over medium-high heat, add scallions and mushrooms, and sauté 1 to 2 minutes, or until scallions wilt and mushrooms soften. Using slotted spatula, transfer scallions and mushrooms to small bowl.

7. Increase heat under skillet to high and add broth, cream, mustard, sherry, hot pepper sauce, and additional ground pepper to taste. Boil vigorously about 4 minutes, or until liquid is reduced to a very thick sauce.

8. Meanwhile, cut four 16 by 12-inch sheets of aluminum foil. Place a fish steak on each and season with salt and pepper. Finely chop enough ham to measure 2 tablespoons. Top each fish steak with equal amounts of carrot, green beans, scallions, and mushrooms.

9. Taste sauce and add salt, if desired. Spoon sauce over vegetables, top with ham, and fold up edges of foil to seal tightly. Refrigerate packets until needed.

10. Twenty minutes before serving, preheat oven to 350 degrees.

11. Place foil packets on 17 by 11-inch baking sheet and bake 10 to 12 minutes.

12. To serve, open foil packets and transfer fish steaks and vegetables to dinner plates. Spoon cooking liquid over fish. Or, serve fish in unopened packets and let guests open them.

ADDED TOUCHES

You will need to begin this recipe at least 9 hours in advance of serving to allow the fruit to absorb the flavors of the cloves and cinnamon.

Spiced Peaches in Red Wine Syrup

4 firm medium-size peaches (1¼ to 1½ pounds
   total weight)
1 cinnamon stick
1½ cups sugar

4 whole cloves
Grated rind of ½ lemon
2 to 3 cups dry red wine

1. Wash and peel peaches. Cut cinnamon stick into 4 pieces.

2. In nonaluminum saucepan large enough to hold peaches in a single layer, combine cinnamon, sugar, cloves, lemon peel, and 2 cups water. Bring to a boil over high heat and boil 10 minutes, or until liquid is syrupy. Turn off heat and immediately add peaches. Weight peaches with plate to keep them submerged, cover, and let stand at room temperature at least 8 hours.

3. One hour before serving, transfer peaches to large bowl; reserve syrup. Pour wine over peaches to cover and weight peaches with plate to keep them submerged. Let stand 1 hour.

4. To serve, using slotted spoon, remove peaches from wine; reserve wine. Cut peaches into ½-inch-thick wedges; discard pits. Arrange slices in pinwheel pattern on individual dessert plates. In small bowl, combine ¼ cup reserved wine with ½ cup reserved syrup and spoon over peaches. Garnish each plate with piece of cinnamon stick.

Sweet Spanish cream sherry is the major flavoring ingredient for this dessert. Be sure to use sweet sherry, which is a dessert wine, rather than dry, or *fino*, sherry in this recipe.

Ice Cream with Sherried Raisins and Toasted Almonds

¼ cup plus 2 tablespoons raisins
¼ cup plus 2 tablespoons Spanish cream sherry
¼ cup slivered blanched almonds
1 pint good-quality vanilla ice cream, softened

1. In small saucepan, combine raisins and sherry and bring to a boil over high heat. Reduce heat to low and simmer, covered, 5 minutes, or until all liquid has been absorbed. Remove pan from heat and let sherried raisins cool at least 10 minutes.

2. Meanwhile, place almonds on small baking sheet and toast in preheated 350-degree oven 3 to 5 minutes, or until light golden. Set aside to cool at least 10 minutes.

3. Fold cooled raisins and almonds into softened ice cream and return to freezer until ice cream is firm.

Chicken in Almond Sauce
Rice with Pimientos and Peas
Composed Vegetable Salad

Chicken in almond sauce and rice with pimientos and peas are served with an impressive salad of raw and steamed vegetables.

The Spanish-style baked rice with pimientos and peas calls for a short-grain rice, such as California pearl, Spanish, or Italian Arborio rice. Short-grain rice has a nutty flavor and a chewy texture quite different from the long-grain varieties. Follow the cooking instructions and timing closely because short-grain rice becomes mushy when overcooked. If short-grain rice is unavailable, you may substitute long-grain rice, but adjust the amount of cooking liquid according to the package directions.

WHAT TO DRINK

This meal could be served with either a medium-bodied white wine, such as California Sauvignon Blanc, or a light red Spanish claret or California Gamay Beaujolais.

SHOPPING LIST AND STAPLES

3½-pound frying chicken, cut into 8
    to 10 pieces
1½ ounces cured ham, such as prosciutto
Small bunch broccoli
Small head romaine or escarole
¼ pound small to medium-size white
    mushrooms
¼ pound snow peas
Small bunch spinach, or small head Belgian
    endive
½ pint cherry tomatoes
Small tomato
Small bunch scallions
Medium-size onion
2 large cloves garlic
Small bunch parsley
1 tablespoon unsalted butter
10-ounce package frozen peas
2¼ cups chicken stock, preferably homemade (see
    page 10), or canned, approximately
5 tablespoons good-quality olive oil
¼ cup fruity olive oil
4 teaspoons sherry vinegar, or 2 tablespoons red wine
    vinegar
¼ pound small French or Italian oil-cured black olives
2-ounce jar chopped or whole pimientos, preferably
    Spanish
2-ounce tin rolled anchovies with capers (optional)
⅓ cup all-purpose flour
1-pound package short-grain rice, such as California
    pearl rice, imported Spanish rice, or Italian Arborio
    rice
2½-ounce package whole blanched almonds
1 tablespoon pine nuts
1 bay leaf
¼ teaspoon dried thyme
Pinch of saffron threads
Salt
Freshly ground pepper
½ cup dry white wine

UTENSILS

Food processor or blender
Large deep nonaluminum skillet with cover
Deep flameproof casserole with cover
Large saucepan with cover
Collapsible vegetable steamer
Small baking sheet
Colander
Salad spinner (optional)
Measuring cups and spoons
Chef's knife
Paring knife
2 wooden spoons
Small jar with tight-fitting lid

START-TO-FINISH STEPS

The Morning of Serving
1. Follow chicken recipe step 1 and rice recipe step 1.
2. Wash and dry parsley. Finely chop enough parsley to measure 2 tablespoons for chicken recipe and 1 tablespoon for rice recipe.
3. Follow chicken recipe step 2.
4. Follow salad recipe step 1.
5. Follow chicken recipe steps 3 through 6.
6. While chicken is cooking, follow rice recipe steps 2 and 3 and salad recipe steps 2 through 4.
7. Follow chicken recipe step 7.

Thirty Minutes Before Serving
1. Follow rice recipe step 4 and chicken recipe step 8.
2. Follow rice recipe step 5 and chicken recipe step 9.
3. While rice and chicken are cooking, follow salad recipe step 5.
4. Follow rice recipe step 6.
5. Follow chicken recipe step 10, rice recipe step 7, salad recipe step 6, and serve.

RECIPES

Chicken in Almond Sauce

3½-pound frying chicken, cut into 8 to 10 pieces
½ ounce whole blanched almonds (about 8)
1 tablespoon pine nuts
⅓ cup all-purpose flour
1 tablespoon unsalted butter
2 tablespoons good-quality olive oil
Medium-size onion
2 large cloves garlic
Small tomato
1½ ounces cured ham, such as prosciutto
½ cup dry white wine
¾ cup chicken stock, approximately
2 tablespoons finely chopped parsley
1 bay leaf
Salt

Freshly ground pepper
¼ pound small to medium-size white mushrooms

1. Preheat oven to 350 degrees. Rinse chicken and dry with paper towels.
2. Place almonds and pine nuts on small baking sheet and toast in oven 3 to 5 minutes, or until light golden; set aside.
3. Dust chicken pieces with flour. Heat butter in oil in large deep nonaluminum skillet over medium-high heat until butter melts. Add chicken and cook, turning with tongs, 7 to 8 minutes, or until brown on all sides.
4. Meanwhile, peel onion and garlic. Coarsely chop onion; mince garlic. Peel tomato, if desired, and chop coarsely. Finely chop enough ham to measure 2 to 3 tablespoons; set aside.
5. Transfer chicken to platter. Add onion and garlic to skillet and sauté over medium-high heat 2 minutes, or until onion wilts. Add tomato and cook 1 minute, or until softened. Return chicken to skillet. Turn off heat.
6. Place nuts in food processor or blender and grind finely. With machine running, gradually add wine and stock and process until as smooth as possible. Pour mixture into skillet and stir in ham, 1 tablespoon parsley, bay leaf, and salt and pepper to taste. Cover skillet and cook chicken over medium-low heat 30 minutes.
7. Remove skillet from heat and set chicken aside at room temperature for up to 6 hours, or refrigerate until 30 minutes before serving.
8. Thirty minutes before serving, wipe mushrooms clean with damp paper towels. Trim stems, and halve mushrooms if large.
9. Add mushrooms to skillet and cook over medium-low heat 20 minutes, or until chicken is heated through, adding a little more stock or water if sauce is too thick.
10. Arrange chicken pieces on serving platter and top with sauce. Sprinkle with remaining tablespoon parsley and serve.

Rice with Pimientos and Peas

10-ounce package frozen peas
Small bunch scallions
2-ounce jar chopped or whole pimientos, preferably
    Spanish
3 tablespoons good-quality olive oil
1 cup short-grain rice, such as California pearl rice,
    imported Spanish rice, or Italian Arborio rice
1 tablespoon finely chopped parsley
¼ teaspoon dried thyme
Pinch of saffron threads
1½ cups chicken stock
Salt

1. Separate ¼ cup frozen peas and let thaw at room temperature; reserve remaining peas for another use.
2. Wash and trim scallions and dry with paper towels. Finely chop enough scallions to measure 2 tablespoons. Drain pimientos and, if necessary, chop enough to measure 2 tablespoons.

3. Heat oil in deep flameproof casserole over medium heat. Add scallions and sauté 1 minute, or until wilted. Add rice and stir until well coated with oil. Add peas, pimientos, parsley, thyme, and saffron. Cover casserole and set rice aside at room temperature until 30 minutes before serving.
4. Thirty minutes before serving, preheat oven to 400 degrees.
5. Add stock, salt to taste, and ¼ cup plus 2 tablespoons water to rice and bring to a boil over high heat. Cover casserole, place in oven, and bake 15 minutes.
6. Remove casserole from oven and let stand, covered, 10 minutes.
7. To serve, turn rice onto serving platter and fluff with fork.

Composed Vegetable Salad

¼ pound snow peas
Small bunch broccoli
12 cherry tomatoes
Small head romaine or escarole
Small bunch spinach, or small head Belgian
    endive
¼ cup fruity olive oil
4 teaspoons sherry vinegar, or 2 tablespoons
    red wine vinegar
Salt
Freshly ground pepper
12 small French or Italian oil-cured black olives
2-ounce tin rolled anchovies with capers
    (optional)

1. Wash snow peas, broccoli, and cherry tomatoes. Trim and string snow peas. Cut broccoli into small florets; reserve remaining broccoli for another use. Remove stems from tomatoes, if necessary.
2. Bring 1 inch water to a boil in large saucepan fitted with vegetable steamer. Place snow peas and broccoli in steamer, cover pan, and cook about 2 minutes, or until vegetables are crisp-tender. Turn vegetables into colander and rinse under cold running water. Drain well, place vegetables in separate plastic bags, and refrigerate until needed.
3. Wash lettuce and spinach or endive and dry in salad spinner or with paper towels. Stack leaves and thinly slice enough combined greens to measure 3 to 4 cups. Place shredded greens in plastic bag and refrigerate until needed. Reserve remaining greens for another use.
4. For vinaigrette, combine oil, vinegar, and salt and pepper to taste in small jar with tight-fitting lid. Shake well. Set aside at room temperature until needed.
5. To serve, make bed of shredded greens on large platter. Arrange a circle of snow peas on top of lettuce. Place cherry tomatoes in a circle on top of snow peas and fill center with broccoli and olives. Drain 4 anchovies, if using.
6. Shake vinaigrette to recombine and pour over salad. Garnish salad with anchovies, if desired.

Susan Wyler

Although she enjoys many different cuisines, Susan Wyler admits to a particular fondness for French cooking. "When I was learning how to cook," she says, "I pored over Julia Child's books, fascinated by the French cooking techniques and the logic of the recipes." To augment her cooking education, Susan Wyler has traveled widely throughout France, sampling the best of its regional dishes and some nontraditional creations as well.

Back in her own New York kitchen, she tends to simplify French recipes to save time, and often experiments with unusual ingredients and flavor combinations. Her Menu 3 is a traditional Provençal dinner filled with the tantalizing aromas of garlic, olives, and herbs. For extra color and flavor in the chicken dish, she adds Italian *pumate*, or sun-dried tomatoes. Garlicky scallops and buttered egg noodles with pine nuts complement the chicken.

Menu 1, a meatless meal the whole family will enjoy, features a gratin of eggplant with red bell peppers and goat cheese that can be prepared entirely in advance, then baked shortly before dinnertime. Nutty *couscous* (a dish the French acquired from the North Africans) and a tossed salad are the accompaniments.

Menu 2 presents a homey carrot and leek soup made more elegant by the addition of ginger (a popular *nouvelle cuisine* ingredient). The beautiful composed salad of roast beef, potatoes, and green beans can be served with or after the soup.

Goat cheese gives the gratin of eggplant and red peppers a distinctive tang. Couscous with caramelized onions and a colorful salad are the side dishes.

Gratin of Eggplant with Red Peppers and Goat Cheese
Couscous with Browned Onions
Tossed Salad

The eggplant gratin calls for Montrachet, a creamy log-shaped goat cheese that is milder than many chèvres. Montrachet comes plain, or rolled in herbs or in finely powdered ash, which gives it a slightly salty taste. You should use the plain variety for this recipe.

WHAT TO DRINK

Any light, dry wine would go well with this menu. A good choice is a French rosé or Beaujolais or a dry California Chenin Blanc.

SHOPPING LIST AND STAPLES

Large eggplant (about 2 pounds)
2 large red bell peppers (about 1 pound total weight)
Small head Boston lettuce
Small head curly leaf lettuce
Large head Belgian endive
1 pint cherry tomatoes
Small cucumber, preferably Kirby
2 medium-size onions
Small red onion
2 medium-size cloves garlic
Small bunch parsley
Small lemon
2 tablespoons unsalted butter
6 ounces Montrachet or other mild, creamy goat cheese
2 ounces Parmesan cheese, preferably imported
1 cup chicken stock, preferably homemade (see page 10), or canned
½ cup plus 1 tablespoon extra-virgin olive oil
2 tablespoons light olive oil
1 tablespoon balsamic vinegar
1-pound package couscous
2½-ounce package sliced almonds
⅓ cup fresh bread crumbs
1 teaspoon herbes de Provence
2 teaspoons kosher salt
Salt
Freshly ground black pepper

UTENSILS

Food processor (optional)
Large heavy-gauge skillet with cover
Small skillet
10- to 12-inch gratin or baking dish
17 x 11-inch heavy-gauge baking sheet
2 small bowls
Colander
Salad spinner (optional)
Measuring cups and spoons
Chef's knife
Paring knife
Wooden spoon
Long-handled two-pronged fork
Grater (if not using food processor)
Metal tongs
Basting brush
Small paper bag

START-TO-FINISH STEPS

The Day Before or the Morning of Serving
1. Follow gratin recipe steps 1 through 4.
2. While peppers are steaming, follow salad recipe step 1 and couscous recipe step 1.
3. While onions are browning, follow gratin recipe steps 5 and 6.
4. Follow couscous recipe step 2 and gratin recipe steps 7 through 10.

Thirty Minutes Before Serving
1. Follow gratin recipe step 11 and salad recipe steps 2 and 3.
2. Follow gratin recipe step 12.
3. While gratin bakes, follow couscous recipe steps 3 through 5 and salad recipe step 4.
4. Follow couscous recipe step 6 and serve with gratin and salad.

RECIPES

Gratin of Eggplant with Red Peppers and Goat Cheese

Large eggplant (about 2 pounds)
2 large red bell peppers (about 1 pound total weight)
2 medium-size cloves garlic
2 ounces Parmesan cheese, preferably imported
2 teaspoons kosher salt
6 tablespoons extra-virgin olive oil

1 teaspoon herbes de Provence
⅓ cup fresh bread crumbs
6 ounces Montrachet or other mild, creamy goat cheese
Freshly ground black pepper

1. Preheat broiler.
2. Wash eggplant and bell peppers and dry with paper towels. Peel and crush garlic. Using food processor or grater, grate enough Parmesan to measure ⅓ cup; set aside.
3. Trim but do not peel eggplant and cut lengthwise into ½-inch-thick slices. Place in colander and sprinkle on both sides with kosher salt. Allow to drain at least 30 minutes.
4. Meanwhile, roast peppers: Spear peppers through top with long-handled two-pronged fork and hold directly over flame of gas burner, or place peppers under broiler, and roast, turning to char skins evenly. Transfer to paper bag and set aside to steam about 10 minutes.
5. Remove peppers from bag and, holding each under cold running water, gently rub off blackened skin. Dry peppers with paper towels. Halve peppers lengthwise and remove stem and seeds. Cut each half in half again and set aside.
6. In small bowl, combine 4 tablespoons olive oil, herbes de Provence, and garlic.
7. Pat eggplant slices dry and press between paper towels to remove as much moisture as possible. Brush slices on both sides with olive oil mixture and place in single layer on 17 x 11-inch heavy-gauge baking sheet. Broil eggplant about 4 inches from heat, turning once with tongs, 10 minutes, or until browned outside and tender and creamy inside.
8. Grease bottom and sides of 10- to 12-inch gratin or baking dish with 1½ teaspoons olive oil. Sprinkle 2 tablespoons bread crumbs over bottom and sides of dish. Halve eggplant slices crosswise on the diagonal and place half of slices in single layer in bottom of dish.
9. Cover eggplant with bell pepper pieces. Cut goat cheese into ¼-inch-thick slices and arrange on top of peppers. Season to taste with black pepper and cover with remaining eggplant.
10. Sprinkle remaining bread crumbs and the Parmesan over top and drizzle with remaining 1½ tablespoons olive oil. Refrigerate, covered, until 30 minutes before serving.
11. Thirty minutes before serving, preheat oven to 375 degrees.
12. Bake gratin, uncovered, 15 to 20 minutes, or until heated through and brown and crusty on top. (If top begins to brown too quickly during cooking, cover loosely with foil.)

Couscous with Browned Onions

2 medium-size onions
2 tablespoons unsalted butter
2 tablespoons light olive oil
Small bunch parsley
1 cup chicken stock
1 cup couscous

¼ cup sliced almonds
Salt and freshly ground pepper

1. Peel onions and chop coarsely. In large heavy-gauge skillet, melt butter in 1 tablespoon oil over medium heat. Add onions, reduce heat to medium-low, and cook, stirring frequently, 10 to 15 minutes, or until golden brown.
2. Remove pan from heat, transfer onions to small bowl, cover, and refrigerate until 15 minutes before serving.
3. Fifteen minutes before serving, wash parsley and dry with paper towels. Finely chop enough parsley to measure 1 teaspoon; reserve remaining parsley for another use.
4. Reheat onions in large skillet over medium-low heat. Add stock and ½ cup water and bring to a boil. Stir in couscous, cover, and remove from heat. Allow to stand 5 minutes.
5. Meanwhile, in small skillet, toast almonds in remaining 1 tablespoon oil over medium heat 2 to 3 minutes, or until golden brown. Add almonds to couscous and stir to combine.
6. Transfer couscous to serving dish, add salt and pepper to taste, and sprinkle with parsley.

Tossed Salad

Small head Boston lettuce
Small head curly leaf lettuce
1 pint cherry tomatoes
Small cucumber, preferably Kirby
Large head Belgian endive
Small lemon
Small red onion
1 tablespoon balsamic vinegar
3 tablespoons extra-virgin olive oil
Salt and freshly ground pepper

1. Separate leaves of Boston and curly leaf lettuce. Wash and dry in salad spinner or with paper towels. Tear lettuce into bite-size pieces. Wrap in paper towels, place in plastic bag, and refrigerate until needed.
2. Thirty minutes before serving, wash and dry tomatoes, cucumber, and endive. Remove stems from tomatoes, if necessary. Peel cucumber and cut crosswise into ¼-inch-thick slices. Cut endive crosswise into ½-inch-wide pieces. Place tomatoes, cucumber, and endive in salad bowl.
3. Halve lemon and squeeze enough juice to measure 2 teaspoons; set aside.
4. Peel onion, cut into ¼-inch-thick slices, and separate slices into rings. Add lettuce and onion rings to salad bowl. Sprinkle with lemon juice, vinegar, and olive oil, and toss well. Season with salt and pepper to taste and toss again.

Boston lettuce

Creamy Carrot Soup
Cold Beef Salad with Shallot-Caper Sauce
French Potato Salad

A velvety vegetable soup garnished with parsley and carrot strips is an elegant partner for the beef and potato salads.

The ingredients in the colorful salads can be precooked and readied for assembly the day before or the morning of serving. Because the potatoes are dressed with a vinaigrette, they will keep well at room temperature without spoiling (the acid in the vinegar acts as a preservative). Accompany the salads with a good crusty French bread, and follow the meal with a cheese such as Stilton, Bleu d'Auvergne, or Camembert, if you like.

WHAT TO DRINK

The cook suggests either a simple red Côtes du Rhône or a California Pinot Noir with these dishes.

SHOPPING LIST AND STAPLES

2 pounds fillet of beef (in one piece), trimmed and tied
5 medium-size red potatoes (about 1½ pounds total weight)
6 to 8 carrots (about 1 pound total weight)
½ pound green beans
Large bunch arugula
Large tomato
2 small leeks, or 2 small onions (8 to 10 ounces total weight)
Medium-size red onion
3 large shallots
1-inch piece fresh ginger
Small bunch fresh tarragon, or ½ teaspoon dried
Small bunch fresh parsley
½ pint heavy cream
2 tablespoons unsalted butter
4 cups chicken stock, preferably homemade (see page 10), or canned
2-ounce jar imported capers
1 tablespoon light olive oil
¾ cup plus 1 tablespoon extra-virgin olive oil
2 tablespoons sherry vinegar
2 tablespoons white wine vinegar
2 teaspoons Dijon mustard
2 tablespoons all-purpose flour
⅛ teaspoon freshly grated nutmeg

⅛ teaspoon ground coriander (optional)
Pinch of Cayenne pepper
Salt and freshly ground black pepper
Coarsely ground black pepper
3 tablespoons dry white wine
1 tablespoon Cognac

UTENSILS

Food processor or blender
3 large saucepans, 1 with cover
Small roasting pan
Large nonaluminum bowl
Medium-size bowl
2 small bowls, 1 nonaluminum
Colander
Small strainer
Measuring cups and spoons
Chef's knife
Paring knife
Wooden spoon
Rubber spatula
Whisk
Meat thermometer

START-TO-FINISH STEPS

The Day Before or the Morning of Serving

1. Follow beef recipe steps 1 through 3 and potato salad recipe step 1.
2. While potatoes are cooking, follow soup recipe steps 1 through 4.
3. While soup is simmering, follow beef recipe step 4 and potato salad recipe step 2.
4. While potatoes are cooling, follow beef recipe step 5.
5. While beef is roasting, follow potato salad recipe steps 3 and 4 and soup recipe step 5.
6. Follow potato salad recipe steps 5 and 6 and beef recipe steps 6 and 7.

Thirty Minutes Before Serving

1. Follow potato salad recipe step 7, soup recipe step 6, and beef recipe steps 8 through 11.
2. Follow potato salad recipe step 8 and soup recipe steps 7 and 8.
3. While soup is reheating, follow beef recipe step 12.
4. Follow soup recipe step 9 and serve with beef salad and potato salad.

RECIPES

Creamy Carrot Soup

2 small leeks, or 2 small onions (8 to 10 ounces total weight)
6 to 8 carrots (about 1 pound total weight)
1-inch piece fresh ginger
2 tablespoons unsalted butter
1 tablespoon light olive oil
2 tablespoons all-purpose flour
4 cups chicken stock
⅛ teaspoon freshly grated nutmeg
⅛ teaspoon ground coriander (optional)
Pinch of Cayenne pepper
2 sprigs parsley
½ cup heavy cream
Salt

1. If using leeks, trim roots and all but 2 to 3 inches of green. Split leeks lengthwise and wash thoroughly under cold running water to remove all grit. If using onions, halve and peel. Coarsely chop leeks or onions.
2. Wash, dry, peel, and trim carrots. Coarsely chop enough carrots to measure 3 cups. Refrigerate remaining carrots for garnish. Peel ginger and finely chop enough to measure 2½ tablespoons.
3. Melt butter in oil in large saucepan over medium heat. Add leeks or onions and cook, stirring occasionally, 5 minutes, or until softened and just beginning to brown. Sprinkle with flour and cook, stirring, 1 minute. Do not allow flour to brown.
4. Stir in stock and bring to a boil. Add chopped carrots, ginger, nutmeg, coriander if using, and Cayenne. Reduce heat to medium low, partially cover pan, and simmer 20 minutes.
5. Remove soup from heat. In food processor or blender, purée soup, in batches if necessary, until smooth. Return soup to saucepan, cover, and refrigerate until 30 minutes before serving.
6. Thirty minutes before serving, set out soup to come to room temperature.
7. Cut enough reserved carrots into very thin julienne strips to measure ¼ cup; set aside. Wash and dry parsley and finely chop enough to measure ½ teaspoon; set aside.
8. Reheat soup over medium-low heat. Add cream, and salt to taste, and simmer 5 minutes. Add 3 tablespoons julienned carrots and simmer another 2 minutes.
9. Transfer soup to tureen and garnish with remaining julienned carrots and chopped parsley.

Cold Beef Salad with Shallot-Caper Sauce

2 pounds fillet of beef (in one piece), trimmed and tied
1 tablespoon Cognac
2 large shallots
Salt
Coarsely ground black pepper
½ cup plus 1 tablespoon extra-virgin olive oil
½ pound green beans
Large bunch arugula
Large tomato
Small bunch fresh tarragon, or ½ teaspoon dried
4 sprigs parsley
1 tablespoon imported capers
Medium-size red onion
2 tablespoons sherry vinegar

1 teaspoon Dijon mustard
French Potato Salad (see following recipe)

1. Rub beef with Cognac and place in small roasting pan.
2. Peel and mince 1 shallot and sprinkle over meat. Season meat with ¼ teaspoon salt and ½ teaspoon pepper and rub with 1 tablespoon olive oil. Set aside at room temperature 30 minutes, turning once or twice.
3. Meanwhile, bring 1 quart water and ½ teaspoon salt to a boil in large saucepan. Wash and dry beans. Trim beans and halve crosswise if desired. Add beans to boiling water and cook 3 to 5 minutes, or until just tender but still slightly resistant to the bite. Turn beans into colander and refresh under cold running water. Set aside to drain.
4. Preheat oven to 450 degrees.
5. Place pan with beef over high heat and sear meat, turning often, 5 minutes, or until browned all over. Roast beef in oven 15 to 20 minutes, or until meat thermometer registers 125 to 130 degrees. Meat should be rare.
6. Remove beef from oven, cover pan with aluminum foil, and refrigerate until 30 minutes before serving.
7. Transfer beans to medium-size bowl, cover with plastic, and refrigerate until 30 minutes before serving.
8. Thirty minutes before serving, set out beef and beans to come to room temperature.
9. Meanwhile, wash and dry arugula, tomato, fresh tarragon if using, and parsley. Trim arugula stems; core tomato and cut into ¼-inch-thick slices. Set aside 2 tarragon sprigs for garnish; finely chop enough remaining tarragon to measure 1 tablespoon and enough parsley to measure 2 tablespoons.
10. Drain capers in strainer. Halve and peel onion and cut into ¼-inch-thick slices. Peel and mince remaining shallot.
11. Whisk together vinegar, mustard, and ¼ teaspoon each salt and pepper in small nonaluminum bowl. Whisking constantly, add remaining ½ cup oil in slow, steady stream and whisk until well blended. Add capers, shallot, parsley, and tarragon, and stir well. Add 2 tablespoons dressing to beans and toss to coat.
12. Cut beef into ½-inch-thick slices. Arrange arugula around edge of large platter. Mound French potato salad in center of platter. Lay beef, onion, and tomato slices decoratively around potato salad, and fill in with bunches of green beans. Drizzle a few spoonsful of dressing over beef, onion, and tomato, and garnish with tarragon sprigs if desired. Serve remaining dressing separately.

French Potato Salad

5 medium-size red potatoes (about 1½ pounds total weight)
Salt
3 tablespoons dry white wine
Large shallot
2 tablespoons white wine vinegar
1 teaspoon Dijon mustard
¼ teaspoon freshly ground pepper
¼ cup extra-virgin olive oil
4 sprigs parsley

1. Wash potatoes and place in large saucepan with salted water to cover. Bring to a boil and cook 20 to 25 minutes, or until potatoes are tender.
2. Turn potatoes into colander to drain and cool.
3. When potatoes are cool enough to handle but still quite warm, peel and slice. Place in large nonaluminum bowl and sprinkle with wine.
4. Peel and mince shallot and add to potatoes; toss gently.
5. Whisk together vinegar, mustard, ½ teaspoon salt, and pepper in small bowl. Whisking constantly, add olive oil in a slow, steady stream and whisk until well combined.
6. Pour dressing over potatoes and toss gently to coat. Cover bowl and refrigerate until 30 minutes before serving.
7. Thirty minutes before serving, set out salad to come to room temperature. Wash and finely chop parsley.
8. Add parsley to salad and toss gently.

ADDED TOUCH

Armagnac, the full-bodied brandy from southwestern France, flavors this compote, which holds up to 48 hours. If you cannot buy Armagnac, use Cognac instead.

Apple and Prune Compote with Armagnac

8 ounces pitted prunes (about 1½ cups)
⅓ cup plus 3 tablespoons Armagnac
2 large Golden Delicious apples (about 1 pound total weight)
Small lemon
⅓ cup sugar
2 cinnamon sticks, broken in half
¼ teaspoon vanilla extract
½ cup sliced almonds
1 tablespoon vegetable oil
½ cup crème fraîche (optional)

1. Place prunes and ⅓ cup Armagnac in small bowl and let soak at least 3 hours, stirring occasionally.
2. Peel and core apples. Cut crosswise into ¼-inch-thick rings, then halve rings crosswise to form crescents.
3. Halve lemon and squeeze enough juice to measure 2 teaspoons. Combine 1½ cups water, lemon juice, sugar, and cinnamon sticks in medium-size nonaluminum saucepan and bring to a boil over high heat. Reduce heat so syrup stays at a simmer.
4. Add apples to syrup and simmer uncovered, stirring frequently, 3 to 4 minutes, or until just tender. Remove pan from heat and transfer apples and syrup to large serving bowl.
5. Stir in prunes and Armagnac, remaining 3 tablespoons Armagnac, and vanilla, and allow to cool. Cover bowl and refrigerate 2 hours.
6. Meanwhile, toast almonds in oil in small skillet over medium-high heat until golden brown. Set aside to cool.
7. To serve, spoon compote into dessert dishes, add a few spoonsful of syrup, top with crème fraîche if desired, and sprinkle with almonds.

Scallops in Shallot-Garlic Butter
Chicken with Green Olives and Sun-Dried Tomatoes
Buttered Egg Noodles with Pine Nuts

For a delightful French meal, serve scallops broiled in scallop shells and zesty chicken and olives with noodles.

The sauté of chicken with green olives is a composite of two of the cook's favorite dishes: duck with green olives, a specialty at the bistro Chez Allard in Paris, and *poulet au feu d'enfer* (literally "chicken in Hell's fire"), a recipe popularized by French chef Paul Bocuse. This variation includes oil-packed sun-dried tomatoes, which are sold in bulk and in jars at specialty food stores and Italian groceries. Although they are costly, these flavorful marinated tomatoes are well worth purchasing as a special treat. There are no substitutes.

WHAT TO DRINK

Serve either white or red wine with this meal. For white, try a crisp, dry French Muscadet or California Sauvignon Blanc. For red, French Beaujolais and California Gamay Beaujolais are both good choices.

SHOPPING LIST AND STAPLES

2½- to 3-pound chicken, cut into 8 serving pieces
1 pound sea scallops
4 medium-size shallots
Medium-size clove garlic
Small bunch flat-leaf parsley
2 lemons
1 stick unsalted butter
2¼-ounce jar pitted green olives
2 ounces oil-packed sun-dried tomatoes
2 tablespoons good-quality olive oil
1½ tablespoons white wine vinegar
6 ounces egg noodles, preferably imported
2-ounce jar pine nuts
1 teaspoon cornstarch
½ teaspoon dried thyme
Small bay leaf
Large pinch of Cayenne pepper
Salt and freshly ground pepper
1 cup dry white wine

UTENSILS

12-inch nonaluminum skillet with cover
Small heavy-gauge skillet
Large saucepan
Medium-size saucepan
17 x 11-inch baking sheet
Small bowl
Colander
Strainer
Measuring cups and spoons
Chef's knife
Paring knife
2 wooden spoons
Metal tongs
8 small or 4 large scallop shells, or 4 individual gratin dishes

START-TO-FINISH STEPS

The Day Before or the Morning of Serving

1. Peel and crush garlic for scallops recipe. Peel shallots and mince 2 for scallops recipe and 2 for chicken recipe.
2. Follow chicken recipe steps 1 through 5.
3. While chicken is cooking, follow noodles recipe step 1 and scallops recipe steps 1 and 2.
4. Follow noodles recipe step 2 and scallops recipe step 3.
5. Follow noodles recipe step 3, scallops recipe steps 4 and 5, and chicken recipe steps 6 and 7.

Thirty Minutes Before Serving Main Course

1. Follow scallops recipe steps 6 through 8 and chicken recipe step 8.
2. While chicken is reheating, follow scallops recipe step 9 and serve as first course.
3. Follow noodles recipe step 4 and chicken recipe step 9.
4. Follow noodles recipe step 5 and chicken recipe step 10.
5. Follow noodles recipe step 6, chicken recipe step 11, and serve.

RECIPES

Scallops in Shallot-Garlic Butter

5 tablespoons unsalted butter
Small bunch flat-leaf parsley
2 lemons
1 pound sea scallops
2 medium-size shallots, minced
Medium-size clove garlic, peeled and crushed
Salt and freshly ground pepper

1. Using 1 tablespoon butter, grease 8 small scallop shells, 4 large scallop shells, or 4 individual gratin dishes.
2. Wash and dry parsley. Refrigerate 8 sprigs for garnish. Finely chop enough remaining parsley to measure 2 teaspoons. Halve 1 lemon and squeeze enough juice to measure 2 teaspoons. Reserve remaining lemon for garnish.
3. Place scallops in colander and rinse under cold water; drain and dry. Cut scallops crosswise into ¼-inch-thick slices. Arrange slices in buttered scallop shells or gratin dishes. Sprinkle scallops with 1 teaspoon lemon juice.
4. Melt remaining butter in small heavy-gauge skillet over medium-low heat. Add shallots and cook 1 minute, or until beginning to soften. Add garlic and cook about 1 minute, or until fragrant. Remove from heat and stir in chopped parsley and remaining 1 teaspoon lemon juice. Season with salt and pepper to taste.
5. Spoon butter mixture over scallops. Place shells on baking sheet, cover, and refrigerate until needed.
6. Just before serving, preheat broiler.
7. Meanwhile, wash reserved lemon and dry with paper towel. Cut lemon into 8 wedges.
8. Place baking sheet with shells about 6 inches from heat and broil 5 minutes, or until scallops are just opaque and tops are lightly browned.
9. Garnish with lemon wedges and parsley and serve.

Chicken with Green Olives and Sun-Dried Tomatoes

2 ounces oil-packed sun-dried tomatoes
2¼-ounce jar pitted green olives
2½- to 3-pound chicken, cut into 8 serving pieces
Salt and freshly ground pepper
2 tablespoons good-quality olive oil
2 medium-size shallots, minced
1½ tablespoons white wine vinegar
1 cup dry white wine
½ teaspoon dried thyme
Small bay leaf
Large pinch of Cayenne pepper
1 teaspoon cornstarch

1. Bring 2 cups water to a boil in medium-size saucepan over high heat.
2. Meanwhile, drain tomatoes in strainer. Cut tomatoes into ½-inch pieces. Turn tomatoes into small bowl; set aside. Rinse strainer. Turn olives into strainer to drain.
3. Place olives in pan of boiling water and blanch 2 minutes. Return olives to strainer, refresh under cold running water, and drain well.
4. Season chicken with salt and pepper. Heat oil in 12-inch nonaluminum skillet over medium-high heat until hot. Add chicken in single layer and cook, turning occasionally, 5 minutes, or until browned lightly on both sides. Pour off fat, leaving only thin film on bottom of pan.
5. Lower heat to medium and return skillet to heat. Add shallots and cook 2 minutes, or until softened but not browned. Add tomatoes, olives, vinegar, wine, ½ cup water, thyme, bay leaf, and Cayenne. Bring mixture to a boil, reduce heat to medium-low, and simmer, covered, turning chicken once or twice, 20 to 25 minutes, or until chicken is tender but not dry.
6. Using tongs, transfer chicken to large platter and cover with foil. Increase heat to medium-high and boil pan juices, scraping bottom of skillet with wooden spoon to incorporate any browned bits, 7 to 10 minutes, or until sauce is reduced to 1 cup. Adjust seasonings.
7. Return chicken and any accumulated juices to skillet. Cover and refrigerate until 20 minutes before serving.
8. Twenty minutes before serving, reheat chicken, covered, over medium-low heat 15 minutes, or until heated through.
9. Leaving sauce in skillet, transfer chicken to serving platter and cover with foil.
10. Stir cornstarch into ½ cup water. Increase heat under sauce to high and bring sauce to a boil. Add cornstarch mixture, reduce heat to medium and, stirring constantly, simmer 1 to 2 minutes.
11. Season sauce with pepper to taste and pour over chicken. Divide among 4 dinner plates.

Buttered Egg Noodles with Pine Nuts

Salt
6 ounces egg noodles, preferably imported
3 tablespoons unsalted butter
3 tablespoons pine nuts
Freshly ground pepper

1. Bring 1½ quarts water and ½ teaspoon salt to a boil in large saucepan over high heat.
2. Add noodles to boiling water and cook 5 to 7 minutes, or until just tender to the bite.
3. Drain noodles in colander and rinse briefly under cold water. Shake colander to drain well. Return noodles to saucepan and add enough cold water to cover by 1 inch. Cover pan and refrigerate until 10 minutes before serving.
4. Ten minutes before serving, reheat noodles over medium heat 3 to 4 minutes, or just until hot. Immediately drain noodles in colander.
5. Melt butter in same saucepan over medium heat. Add pine nuts and sauté, stirring, 2 to 3 minutes, or until golden brown.
6. Return noodles to pan and toss until warmed and coated with butter. Season with salt and pepper to taste and divide among 4 dinner plates.

ADDED TOUCH

This classic pear and ice cream dessert makes a refreshing conclusion to a rich, spicy meal.

Poires Belle Hélène

Small lemon
2 firm ripe pears, preferably Bartlett or Anjou (about 1 pound total weight)
½ cup sugar
½ vanilla bean, split, or 1 teaspoon vanilla extract
3½ ounces bittersweet or dark sweet chocolate, preferably imported
2 tablespoons unsalted butter
1 tablespoon Cognac
1 pint good-quality vanilla ice cream
Candied violets (optional)

1. Squeeze enough lemon juice to measure 1 teaspoon.
2. Peel pears, cut in half, and core.
3. Combine 1 cup water, sugar, vanilla bean or extract, and lemon juice in wide medium-size nonaluminum saucepan. Bring to a boil over medium heat, stirring, and cook 2 minutes. Reduce heat so syrup stays at a simmer.
4. Add pears, partially cover pan, and poach pears, turning occasionally, 10 to 15 minutes, or until just tender. Remove pan from heat and allow pears to cool in syrup.
5. When pears are cool, cover pan and refrigerate at least 1 hour.
6. Melt chocolate with butter in small heavy-gauge saucepan over very low heat. Stir in Cognac. Remove sauce from heat and allow to cool, then cover and refrigerate until ready to serve.
7. Just before serving, reheat sauce over low heat. Scoop ice cream into 4 dessert dishes. Top with pear halves and warm sauce. Garnish with candied violets, if desired.

Michael McLaughlin

MENU 1 (Right)
Marinated Seafood with Linguine
Julienned Vegetables
Italian Bread with Gorgonzola Butter

MENU 2
Fricassee of Chicken with Paprika
Noodles and Cabbage with Dill

MENU 3
Sausage, Mushroom, and Lentil Gratin
Winter Greens with Mustard Dressing

Despite a particular passion for chili and everything spicy, Michael McLaughlin still loves foods of every description. His three make-ahead menus can best be described as eclectic, but all are structured according to his fundamental rules of meal planning: Suit the menu to the season; let the hour of eating dictate the complexity of the dishes; and glamorize the familiar.

For instance, Menu 1 is an ideal late-evening summer party. It features an Italian-inspired cold marinated seafood salad tossed with hot linguine, which is easy to prepare and also "sensual eating," according to the cook. A sauté of julienned vegetables makes a colorful partner for the seafood and functions as a warm salad. The grilled bread with Gorgonzola butter is served hot and bubbling from the oven.

Menu 2, satisfying fare for a casual Sunday supper, is a stick-to-the-ribs American meal with Middle European overtones. It features the American classic, chicken fricassee, flavored here with leeks and Hungarian paprika. The chicken is offered on a bed of noodles mixed with sautéed cabbage.

Perfect for a fall or winter evening, Menu 3 beckons friends to eat before the fire or in a warm and cozy kitchen. The one-dish main course, a French peasant gratin, is a hearty combination of sausages, mushrooms, and lentils. The salad of winter greens adds texture and a welcome bit of tartness.

A salad of cold marinated seafood tossed with hot linguine and paired with colorful sautéed peppers, carrots, and squash is an elegant hot-weather meal. Gorgonzola butter coats the Italian bread.

Marinated Seafood with Linguine
Julienned Vegetables
Italian Bread with Gorgonzola Butter

Ideally, the seafood for the pasta dish should be prepared the day before serving to allow the raw scallops and shrimp to "cook" completely in the vinegar marinade. This heatless cooking method keeps the seafood especially moist. The small amount of heat the marinated seafood receives when combined with the hot pasta brings out the flavors of the oil, vinegar, and herbs.

If you can find it, use an imported Italian Gorgonzola for the grilled bread. Select a sweet, or *dolcelatte*, cheese, which is milder and creamier than aged Gorgonzola. Once the bread has been spread with the savory butter, it requires only a minute or two under the broiler to brown.

WHAT TO DRINK

The cook recommends relaxed "picnic" wines with this menu: A California white Zinfandel or Chenin Blanc, or an Italian Soave, would all be good.

SHOPPING LIST AND STAPLES

¾ pound medium-size shrimp
¾ pound bay scallops
2 medium-size tomatoes (about 1 pound total weight)
3 medium-size carrots (about ½ pound total weight)
Large red bell pepper
Large green bell pepper
Medium-size zucchini
Medium-size yellow squash
Small red onion
Medium-size clove garlic
Small bunch each mint, coriander, and flat-leaf parsley
7 tablespoons unsalted butter
¼ pound Gorgonzola cheese, preferably imported
1¼ cups extra-virgin olive oil, approximately
½ cup plus 2 tablespoons red wine vinegar, preferably imported
1 pound linguine, preferably imported
Large loaf Italian bread
Salt and freshly ground black pepper

UTENSILS

Food processor or blender
Large stockpot
10-inch skillet
Baking sheet
Medium-size nonaluminum bowl
Small bowl
Colander
Measuring cups and spoons
Chef's knife
Bread knife
Paring knife
2 wooden spoons
Slotted spoon
Rubber spatula
Pastry brush

START-TO-FINISH STEPS

The Day Before Serving
Thirty minutes ahead: Set out butter and Gorgonzola to come to room temperature for bread recipe.
1. Follow seafood recipe steps 1 and 2.
2. Follow vegetables recipe step 1.
3. Follow bread recipe steps 1 and 2.

Thirty Minutes Before Serving
1. Follow bread recipe step 3 and seafood recipe steps 3 through 7.
2. Follow bread recipe steps 4 and 5, vegetables recipe step 2, and seafood recipe step 8.
3. While pasta is cooking, follow vegetables recipe steps 3 through 5.
4. Follow seafood recipe step 9, bread recipe step 6, and serve with vegetables.

RECIPES

Marinated Seafood with Linguine

¾ pound medium-size shrimp
¾ pound bay scallops
½ cup plus 2 tablespoons red wine vinegar, preferably imported
Small bunch mint
Small bunch coriander
2 medium-size tomatoes (about 1 pound total weight)
Small red onion
⅔ cup extra-virgin olive oil
1 tablespoon salt, approximately
1 pound linguine, preferably imported
Freshly ground black pepper

1. Pinch off legs of shrimp, several at a time, then bend back and snap off sharp, beaklike pieces of shell just above tail. Remove shell, except for tail, and discard. Using sharp paring knife, make shallow incision along back of each shrimp, exposing digestive vein. Extract vein and discard.
2. Combine shrimp, scallops, and ½ cup vinegar in medium-size nonaluminum bowl; stir to combine. Cover bowl and refrigerate overnight, stirring occasionally.
3. Thirty minutes before serving, set out seafood to come to room temperature.
4. Meanwhile, bring 6 quarts water to a boil in large stockpot over high heat.
5. Wash mint and coriander and dry with paper towels. Finely chop enough herbs to measure ½ cup each; set aside.
6. Wash tomatoes and dry with paper towels. Core tomatoes and cut into ½-inch pieces. Peel and finely chop onion.
7. Turn seafood into colander to drain, then transfer to large serving bowl. Add mint, coriander, tomatoes, and onion to bowl. Add olive oil and remaining 2 tablespoons vinegar and toss gently. Set aside.
8. Stir salt into boiling water, add linguine, and cook 8 to 12 minutes, or according to package directions until *al dente*.
9. Turn pasta into colander to drain and immediately add to seafood mixture. Toss well, add salt and pepper to taste, and toss again.

Julienned Vegetables

3 medium-size carrots (about ½ pound total weight)
1 each large red and green bell pepper
Medium-size zucchini
Medium-size yellow squash
3 tablespoons unsalted butter
Salt
3 to 4 tablespoons extra-virgin olive oil
Freshly ground black pepper

1. Wash vegetables and dry with paper towels. Peel and trim carrots. Core and seed bell peppers. Trim zucchini and yellow squash. Cut all vegetables into fine julienne. Place vegetables in separate plastic bags and refrigerate until about 10 minutes before serving.
2. About 10 minutes before serving, melt butter in 10-inch skillet over medium heat. When butter foams, add carrots and sauté, stirring, 4 minutes.
3. Add bell peppers and sauté, stirring, 2 minutes.
4. Add zucchini and yellow squash, and salt to taste, and sauté, stirring, 2 minutes.
5. Using slotted spoon, transfer vegetables to serving dish. Drizzle with olive oil, season generously with pepper, and toss well.

Italian Bread with Gorgonzola Butter

Small bunch flat-leaf parsley
Medium-size clove garlic
¼ pound Gorgonzola cheese, preferably imported, at room temperature
4 tablespoons unsalted butter, at room temperature
Large loaf Italian bread
2 tablespoons extra-virgin olive oil
Freshly ground black pepper

1. Wash and dry parsley. Finely chop enough parsley to measure ½ cup. Crush and peel garlic.
2. Combine parsley, garlic, Gorgonzola, and butter in container of food processor or blender and process until smooth and green. Scrape into small bowl, cover, and refrigerate until 30 minutes before serving.
3. Thirty minutes before serving, set out Gorgonzola butter to come to room temperature.
4. Fifteen minutes before serving, preheat broiler.
5. Halve bread lengthwise. Spread Gorgonzola butter generously down center of each half, leaving ¼-inch border all around. Brush borders with olive oil. Sprinkle bread with pepper and place on baking sheet.
6. Broil bread 4 to 5 inches from heat 1 to 2 minutes, or until bread is crisp and golden brown, and butter is bubbling. Transfer bread to platter or napkin-lined basket.

ADDED TOUCH

This easy ice is made from an unusual blend of citrus juices and fresh basil. Most ice-and-salt type ice cream makers will be unable to freeze the mixture solid. Complete the process in the freezer.

To still-freeze the ice, pour the strained liquid into a shallow metal pan and freeze it for 3 to 4 hours. Stir the mixture with a fork twice during freezing to break up the larger ice crystals. The texture of the still-frozen ice will be more granular than the machine-made version, and the volume will not be as great, but the flavor will be as good.

Orange and Basil Ice

2 large lemons
7 to 10 large juice oranges
Large bunch basil
1¼ cups sugar

1. Halve lemons and squeeze enough juice to measure ½ cup. Halve oranges and squeeze enough juice to measure 3½ cups. Strain juices into small nonaluminum saucepan.
2. Wash and dry basil. Measure 1 cup loosely packed leaves; set aside in medium-size heatproof bowl.
3. Add sugar to juices and bring to a simmer over medium heat, stirring constantly.
4. Pour hot liquid over basil leaves, stir well, and allow to cool. Cover and refrigerate at least 4 hours, or overnight.
5. Pour basil mixture through fine strainer into canister of ice cream freezer and proceed according to manufacturer's instructions. If ice is not firmly frozen, transfer to storage container and freeze, covered, until firm.
6. To serve, soften ice slightly in refrigerator before scooping into sherbet dishes.

Fricassee of Chicken with Paprika
Noodles and Cabbage with Dill

A comforting dinner of chicken fricassee with noodles and sautéed cabbage is a perfect way to end the day with family or friends.

Fricasseeing is an old-fashioned method of preparing chicken that combines two cooking techniques—frying and stewing. The gently cooked chicken is protected during refrigeration by a covering of stock, and so remains moist. The flavors of the dish intensify as it stands.

For the best flavor, season the chicken with imported sweet Hungarian paprika, sold in tins or occasionally in bulk at specialty food stores. The finest paprika is from the town of Szeged and is labeled as such. Coarse-textured Spanish paprika (the usual supermarket variety) is not a substitute. Fresh paprika looks bright red; brown or faded powder is tasteless. Because paprika loses its flavor quickly, store it in a tightly closed jar in the refrigerator.

If you must use dried noodles, start the water boiling earlier to allow for additional cooking time.

WHAT TO DRINK

A delicate, fragrant white wine would be a fine complement to this menu. Try a Riesling from Germany, California, or the Pacific Northwest.

98

SHOPPING LIST AND STAPLES

2½- to 3-pound chicken, cut into 8 serving pieces
Medium-size head green cabbage (about 2 pounds)
4 medium-size leeks (about 1 pound total weight)
Small bunch dill
3 eggs
½ pint heavy cream
1 stick plus 4 tablespoons unsalted butter
3 cups chicken stock, preferably homemade (see page 10), or canned
½ pound fresh flat noodles, such as fettuccine
2 tablespoons sweet paprika, preferably Hungarian
Salt and freshly ground black pepper
1 cup dry white wine

UTENSILS

Large stockpot
2 large skillets with covers

Large bowl
Medium-size bowl
Colander
Measuring cups and spoons
Chef's knife
Paring knife
Wooden spoon
Whisk
Metal tongs

START-TO-FINISH STEPS

The Day Before or the Morning of Serving
1. Follow chicken recipe steps 1 through 4.
2. While chicken simmers, follow noodles recipe step 1.
3. Follow chicken recipe step 5.

Twenty Minutes Before Serving
1. Follow noodles recipe steps 2 and 3 and chicken recipe steps 6 and 7.
2. Follow noodles recipe step 4 and chicken recipe steps 8 and 9.
3. Follow noodles recipe steps 5 and 6, chicken recipe step 10, and serve.

RECIPES

Fricassee of Chicken with Paprika

2½- to 3-pound chicken, cut into 8 serving pieces
4 tablespoons unsalted butter
4 medium-size leeks (about 1 pound total weight)
2 tablespoons sweet paprika, preferably Hungarian
3 cups chicken stock
1 cup dry white wine
Salt and freshly ground black pepper
3 eggs
⅔ cup heavy cream
Noodles and Cabbage with Dill (see following recipe)

1. Rinse and dry chicken. Melt butter in large skillet over medium heat. When butter foams, add chicken, skin-side down, reduce heat to medium-low, and cook, turning often with tongs, 10 minutes. Chicken should not brown.
2. Meanwhile, trim green tops and root ends from leeks. Split leeks lengthwise, wash thoroughly, and dry. Coarsely chop enough leeks to measure 3 cups.
3. Using tongs, transfer chicken to large plate. Add leeks

and paprika to skillet, stir, and cook, covered, 10 minutes.
4. After 10 minutes, stir in stock and wine, return chicken to skillet, and season with salt and pepper to taste. Bring liquid to a boil, reduce heat to medium-low, and simmer, partially covered, 30 minutes, basting often and turning chicken once.
5. Remove skillet from heat and allow chicken to cool in its liquid. Refrigerate chicken and its liquid in skillet until about 20 minutes before serving.
6. Twenty minutes before serving, separate eggs. Place yolks in medium-size bowl; reserve whites for another use.
7. Reheat chicken in skillet, covered, over medium heat, stirring often, until liquid comes to a simmer.
8. Add cream to egg yolks in bowl and whisk to combine. Whisking constantly, add 2 cups hot chicken cooking liquid to yolk mixture in a slow, steady stream.
9. Pour mixture back into skillet, reduce heat to low, and cook, stirring gently and turning chicken occasionally, about 5 minutes, or until sauce thickens. Do not let sauce boil or it will curdle.
10. Serve fricassee over noodles and cabbage with dill.

Noodles and Cabbage with Dill

Medium-size head green cabbage (about 2 pounds)
Small bunch dill
1 stick unsalted butter
1 tablespoon salt, approximately
½ pound fresh flat noodles, such as fettuccine
Freshly ground black pepper

1. Wash and dry cabbage. Remove any tough or wilted leaves. Quarter and core cabbage and cut into ¼-inch-wide shreds. You should have 8 to 9 cups. Place cabbage in plastic bag and refrigerate until 20 minutes before serving.
2. Twenty minutes before serving, bring 4 quarts water to a boil in large stockpot.
3. Meanwhile, wash and dry dill. Finely chop enough dill to measure ¼ cup; set aside.
4. Melt butter in large skillet over medium heat. Add cabbage, and salt to taste, and toss. Cover skillet and cook cabbage 5 minutes, stirring once or twice.
5. Stir 1 tablespoon salt into boiling water, add noodles, and cook 1 minute, or just until water returns to a boil. Immediately turn noodles into colander to drain.
6. Turn noodles and cabbage into large bowl and toss to combine. Add dill, and pepper to taste, and toss again.

Sausage, Mushroom, and Lentil Gratin
Winter Greens with Mustard Dressing

Ward off the cold with this robust fare: Sausages, mushrooms, and lentils served with a crisp green salad and dark beer.

You can use any fully cooked smoked sausage for the main course; the cook prefers a type labeled "hot links," sold in supermarkets. The lentils should be washed before use to remove any bits of debris, but they do not require presoaking.

WHAT TO DRINK

This hearty meal demands beer—dark, light, or amber. You might even want to serve stout.

SHOPPING LIST AND STAPLES

1 pound fully cooked smoked sausage

¾ pound fresh mushrooms
Small head romaine lettuce
Small head chicory
Small bunch watercress
2 medium-size yellow onions (about 1 pound total weight)
3 medium-size cloves garlic
Small bunch parsley
2 lemons
3 eggs
3 tablespoons unsalted butter
2 ounces Parmesan cheese, preferably imported
3 cups chicken stock, preferably homemade (see page 10), or canned

1¼ cups good-quality olive oil
1 cup vegetable oil
5 tablespoons Dijon mustard
1¼ cups brown lentils (about ½ pound)
2 tablespoons dry bread crumbs
1 teaspoon dried thyme
1 bay leaf
Salt and freshly ground black pepper

UTENSILS

Food processor or blender
Medium-size skillet
Large saucepan with cover
1½-quart baking dish
2 small bowls, 1 nonaluminum
Colander
Salad spinner (optional)
Measuring cups and spoons
Chef's knife
Paring knife
Wooden spoon
Slotted spoon
Rubber spatula
Grater (if not using food processor)
Citrus juicer (optional)

START-TO-FINISH STEPS

The Day Before or the Morning of Serving

1. Follow gratin recipe steps 1 through 3 and salad recipe step 1.
2. Follow gratin recipe steps 4 through 8.
3. While lentils are cooking, follow salad recipe steps 2 and 3.
4. Follow gratin recipe steps 9 and 10.

Thirty Minutes Before Serving

1. Follow gratin recipe steps 11 through 13.
2. Follow salad recipe step 4, gratin recipe step 14, and serve.

RECIPES

Sausage, Mushroom, and Lentil Gratin

1 pound fully cooked smoked sausage

¼ cup good-quality olive oil
2 medium-size yellow onions (about 1 pound total weight)
3 medium-size cloves garlic
1 teaspoon dried thyme
1 bay leaf
1¼ cups brown lentils (about ½ pound)
¾ pound fresh mushrooms
3 cups chicken stock
1½ teaspoons salt
Freshly ground black pepper
3 tablespoons unsalted butter
Small bunch parsley
2 ounces Parmesan cheese, preferably imported
2 tablespoons dry bread crumbs

1. Cut sausage into bite-size pieces.
2. Heat 2 tablespoons olive oil in large saucepan over medium-high heat until hot. Add sausage and cook, stirring occasionally, about 10 minutes, or until browned all over.
3. Meanwhile, peel, halve, and coarsely chop onions. Peel and mince garlic.
4. With slotted spoon, transfer sausage to plate.
5. Add onions, garlic, thyme, and bay leaf to saucepan and cook, covered, 10 minutes, stirring occasionally.
6. Meanwhile, rinse lentils in colander and drain. Remove any bits of dirt or debris.
7. Wipe mushrooms clean with damp paper towels. Quarter mushrooms and set aside.
8. Add sausage, stock, lentils, salt, and pepper to taste to saucepan with onions. Bring to a boil, reduce heat slightly, and cook, uncovered, stirring occasionally, 25 minutes, or until lentils are just tender.
9. Ten minutes before lentils are done, melt butter in medium-size skillet over medium heat. When butter foams, add mushrooms and cook, tossing and stirring, 10 minutes, or until tender.
10. Stir mushrooms into lentil mixture. Remove and discard bay leaf. Pour mixture into shallow 1½-quart baking dish. Allow mixture to cool slightly, then cover and refrigerate until needed.
11. Thirty minutes before serving, preheat oven to 400 degrees.
12. Meanwhile, wash parsley and dry with paper towels. Mince enough parsley to measure ¼ cup. In food pro-

cessor, or with grater, grate enough Parmesan to measure 2 tablespoons.

13. Combine parsley, Parmesan, and bread crumbs in small bowl. Sprinkle over lentil mixture and drizzle with 2 tablespoons olive oil. Place baking dish on middle rack of oven and bake 25 minutes, or until lentils are bubbling and top is crisp and brown.

14. Divide gratin among 4 dinner plates and serve.

Winter Greens with Mustard Dressing

Small bunch watercress
Small head romaine lettuce
Small head chicory
3 eggs
2 lemons
5 tablespoons Dijon mustard
Salt and freshly ground black pepper
1 cup good-quality olive oil
1 cup vegetable oil

1. Wash greens and dry in salad spinner or with paper towels. Remove stems from watercress. Remove and discard any bruised or discolored romaine leaves. Remove tough outer chicory leaves. Tear romaine and chicory into bite-size pieces. Place greens in plastic bag and refrigerate until just before serving.

Watercress

2. Separate 1 egg, placing white in container of food processor or blender and reserving yolk for another use. Halve lemons and squeeze enough juice to measure 5 tablespoons.

3. Add remaining 2 eggs, lemon juice, mustard, and salt and pepper to taste to egg white in processor or blender. Process 30 seconds. With machine running, add olive oil, then vegetable oil, in slow, steady stream. Taste, and correct seasonings if necessary. Transfer dressing to small nonaluminum bowl, cover, and refrigerate until just before serving.

4. To serve, place greens in large salad bowl and toss to combine. Mound some salad on each of 4 dinner or salad plates and drizzle with dressing. Serve remaining dressing separately.

────────

ADDED TOUCH

For this dessert, a flavorful syrup of orange juice and white wine is mixed with yogurt to make a tart, creamy sauce. Sprinkle the fruit with crumbled *amaretti*, Italian almond cookies available in specialty food shops. Or, try toasted almonds, orange zest, or a light dusting of powdered cinnamon.

Poached Pears with Yogurt Sauce

Large lemon
7 to 10 large juice oranges
4 large, firm pears, such as Bartlett or Anjou (about 2 pounds total weight)
1 cup dry white wine
½ vanilla bean
1 cup sugar
½ cup plain yogurt
4 amaretti

1. Halve lemon and squeeze enough juice to measure 3 tablespoons. Halve oranges and squeeze enough juice to measure 3 cups.

2. Combine lemon juice and 4 cups cold water in medium-size nonaluminum bowl.

3. Peel, core, and quarter pears, adding them to bowl of acidulated water as they are quartered.

4. Place orange juice, wine, vanilla bean, and sugar in medium-size nonaluminum saucepan and bring to a boil over medium heat, stirring often and skimming froth as necessary. Reduce heat to medium-low and simmer, uncovered, 10 minutes.

5. Drain pears. Add to syrup and simmer, stirring gently, 10 minutes, or until pears are just tender.

6. Using slotted spoon, transfer pears to large heatproof bowl. Simmer syrup another 10 minutes, or until slightly reduced. Pour syrup over pears and allow to come to room temperature. Refrigerate, covered, until serving time.

7. To serve, using slotted spoon, arrange pears decoratively on 4 dessert plates. Whisk ½ cup syrup and yogurt together in small bowl and spoon over pears. Crush amaretti and sprinkle over pears.

Acknowledgments

The Editors would like to thank the following for their courtesy in lending items for photography: *Cover:* linens, platters—Wolfman-Gold & Good Co.; serving spoon—Gorham. *Frontispiece:* tray, tablecloth, napkins—Ad Hoc Housewares; carafe, flatware, plates—Sointu; trolley—The Museum Store of the Museum of Modern Art; milk bottle—Slotnick Collection; refrigerator—White-Westinghouse. *Pages 14–15:* plates, platter, carafe, pitcher—Jenifer Harvey Lang; napkins—Ad Hoc Softwares; flatware—Gorham. *Pages 18–19:* tiles—Country Floors; flatware—Gorham; plates—Columbus Avenue General Store. *Page 21:* tiles—Country Floors; flatware—Gorham. *Pages 24–25:* plates, napkin—Creative Resources. *Page 28:* platters—Gear. *Page 38:* glass—Gorham; flatware—Christofle; plate, bowl, napkins—Frank McIntosh at Henri Bendel. *Page 41:* melon bowl—Amigo Country; basket, woven pad—Be Seated, Inc. *Pages 44–45:* dishes, glasses—Gear; tiles—Nemo Tile; flatware—Gorham. *Page 48:* plates—Gear; tablecloth, napkin—China Seas; fork—Gorham. *Page 51:* tabletop—Formica® Brand Laminate by Formica Corp.; dishes—Pottery Barn; flatware—Sointu. *Pages 54–55:* obi, platter—Japan Interiors Gallery; travertine—Nemo Tile; bowls, chicken platter—Ad Hoc Housewares. *Page 58:* platters—Japan Interiors Gallery.

Page 61: underplate—Phillip Mueller, courtesy of Creative Resources; plate—Creative Resources; napkin—Susskind Collection. *Pages 64–65:* glasses, bowls, platters—Wolfman-Gold & Good Co. *Page 68:* flatware—Gorham; plates—Julien Mousa-Oghli; glasses—Pottery Barn; tabletop—Formica® Brand Laminate by Formica Corp. *Page 71:* dinner plate—Klove Collection; tablecloth—Conran's; basket—Pottery Barn. *Pages 74–75:* plates, glass—Amigo Country. *Page 78:* glass—Amigo Country; dishes—Penelope Casas; spoon—Gorham. *Pages 84–85:* platter, terracotta dishes—Penelope Casas. *Page 88:* platter, tureen—Feu Follet. *Page 91:* tablecloth, napkin, plate, tile, glass—Pierre Deux; fork, shells—Charles Lamalle; napkin ring—Wolfman-Gold & Good Co. *Pages 94–95:* servers, platters, bread tray, tablecloth—Frank McIntosh at Henri Bendel. *Page 98:* plate, napkin—Chelsea Passage at Barney's. *Page 100:* mat, napkin, plate—Chelsea Passage at Barney's; fork—Wallace Silversmiths. *Kitchen equipment courtesy of:* White-Westinghouse, Commercial Aluminum Cookware Co., Robot-Coupe, Caloric, Kitchen-Aid, J.A. Henckels Zwillingswerk, Inc., and Schwabel Corp. Microwave oven compliments of Litton Microwave Cooking Products. Illustrations by Ray Skibinski
Production by Giga Communications

Mail Order Sources

The following suppliers fill some mail orders for special Oriental ingredients. Before ordering, however, it is advisable to call or write for a catalogue or information on products, prices, and terms.

Thai
Bangkok Grocery
Anan Import/Export
805-809 Driggs Avenue
Brooklyn, NY 11211
(718) 384-1188

China Trading Company
271 Crown Street
New Haven, CT 06510
(203) 865-9465

Vietnamese
Vietnam House
242 Farmington Avenue
Hartford, CT 06105
(203) 524-0010

Index

*Time-Life Books Inc. offers a wide
range of fine recordings, including
a Big Band series. For subscription
information, call 1-800-621-7026, or
write TIME-LIFE MUSIC, Time & Life
Building, Chicago, Illinois 60611.*

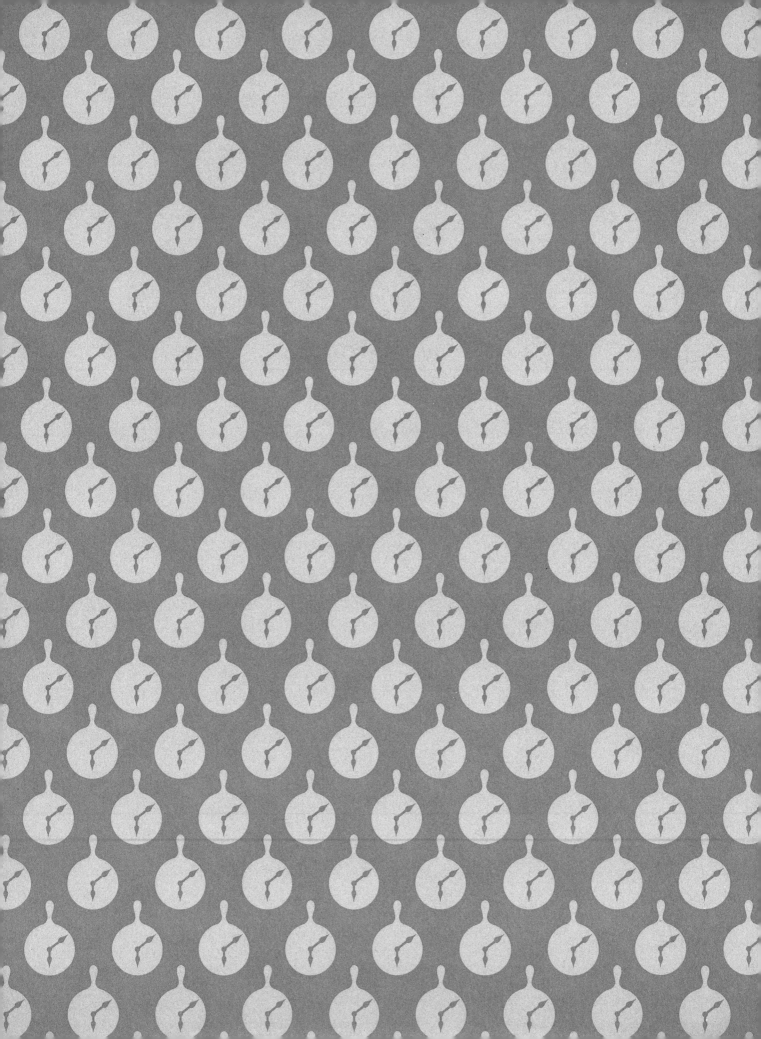